Radio Times
The Sixties

DESIGN & ART DIRECTION
Mark Taylor

EDITOR & RESEARCHER
Patrick Mulkern

HEAD OF HERITAGE
Ralph Montagu

ADDITIONAL PICTURE RESEARCH
Natalie Drewery
David Carlisle

PRODUCTION & AD SERVICES DIRECTOR
Sharon Thompson

PRODUCTION MANAGER
Steve Calver

PUBLISHER Ben Head

PUBLISHING DIRECTOR
Zoe Helme

MANAGING DIRECTOR
Dominic Murray

EDITORS, RADIO TIMES
Shem Law, Tom Loxley

MANAGING EDITOR
Claire Hollingsworth

REPRO by Robert James and Rhapsody

PRINTED by Swan Print

IMAGES SUPPLIED by *Radio Times* Archive, Getty Images, Allstar

DEDICATION
This book is dedicated to the memory of *Radio Times* staff photographer Don Smith (1932–2022)

WITH SPECIAL THANKS to Tony Blackburn, James Burke, Susan Hampshire, Waris Hussein, Ken Loach, Alvin Rakoff and Valerie Singleton

Radio Times would also like to thank all staff members, freelance contributors, writers, photographers and illustrators past and present

RadioTimes

© Immediate Media Company London Limited, 2022
ISBN 978-0-9929364-9-5

LET'S PARTY!
"It's *Crackerjack!*" On the cover of *Radio Times* in 1967, Leslie Crowther, Peter Glaze and two young friends were celebrating the festive season and 12 years of the children's entertainment show

Contents

4 Foreword by Patrick Mulkern

6 1960 TV Centre, *Maigret*, David Attenborough and Kenneth Williams

14 1961 Tony Hancock, Sean Connery and *A for Andromeda*

20 1962 Alvin Rakoff on *Z Cars*, Waris Hussein on *Compact*, plus *The Rag Trade*, *Steptoe and Son* and *Dr Finlay's Casebook*

34 1963 The Beatles, Bob Dylan, *That Was the Week That Was* and *Doctor Who*

42 1964 Daleks, Frankie Howerd, BBC2 and Valerie Singleton on *Blue Peter*

54 1965 *Not Only… but Also*, Muhammad Ali, *The Likely Lads* and *Plays*

64 1966 World Cup, *Till Death Us Do Part*, Ken Loach on *Cathy Come Home*

74 1967 Susan Hampshire on *The Forsyte Saga* and *Vanity Fair*, Tony Blackburn on Radio 1, Jacqueline du Pré

86 1968 Mexico Olympics, kids' classics, *Dad's Army*, Morecambe and Wise, *Top of the Pops*, Sandie Shaw, Joan Bakewell

100 1969 James Burke on the Moon landing; *Star Trek*, *Civilisation*, *The Liver Birds* and John Lennon

Published by Immediate Media Company London Ltd, Vineyard House, 44 Brook Green, London W6 7BT. Published in the United Kingdom 2022. *Radio Times* is part of Immediate Media Company London Ltd. All rights reserved. No part of this publication may be reproduced or transmitted in any form or by any means, electronic or mechanical, including photocopying, recording or any information storage and retrieval system, without prior permission in writing from the publisher. The bookazine is sold subject to the condition that it shall not, by way of trade or otherwise, be lent, resold, hired out or otherwise circulated without the publisher's prior consent in any form of binding or cover other than that in which it is published and without a similar condition including this condition being imposed on the subsequent purchaser.

Radio Times celebrates a golden decade

Hop aboard the Magic Roundabout as we take you to the Moon and back, meeting the Beatles and Daleks along the way…

FOREWORD BY **Patrick Mulkern** EDITOR *RADIO TIMES: THE SIXTIES*

We've all heard the witty adage that if you can remember the 1960s, you weren't really there. Such nonsense might apply to a shrinking number of addled pop-mongers but not to the rest of us who *were* there and vividly recall the key events, luminous personalities and landmark TV and radio shows of that golden decade.

When the Beatles were still pumping out hit after hit… when a barefoot Sandie Shaw won Eurovision with *Puppet on a String*… when a young mother had her children wrenched away from her in *Cathy Come Home*… when Zebedee went "Boing!" every teatime on *The Magic Roundabout*… and when *Dad's Army* was brand new.

Every Friday meant the joy of "It's five to five. It's *Crackerjack!*", while Saturday was an appointment with terror as the Yeti came roaring out of the shadows of the London Underground in Patrick Troughton's *Doctor Who*. And everything stopped in our house twice a week when my busy mum finally put her feet up to watch her favourite soap, *The Newcomers*.

Many will recall where they were when the news broke of JFK's assassination in 1963 and when England beat West Germany in the final of the 1966 World Cup. I was a babe-in-arms but am told that when Geoff Hurst scored the defining goal, my jubilant dad threw me in the air and I nearly hit the ceiling. (This probably accounts for my lifelong aversion to football.) Even now, I can clearly picture 1969, sitting with my dad in front of our temperamental black-and-white Philips telly, building an Airfix model of the Apollo 11 rocket and breathing in Bostik fumes, while the real-life mission to the Moon unfolded hour by hour.

For this special *Radio Times* celebration of the 1960s, we've spoken to some of the talented people who really were there – making all those programmes we remember. Ground-breaking directors Alvin Rakoff, Waris Hussein and Ken Loach. Queen of period drama Susan Hampshire. *Blue Peter* legend Valerie Singleton. Radio 1's Tony Blackburn, who fed us a diet of Flower Power, Motown and his barking dog Arnold while we wolfed down our Ready Brek. And James Burke, who sought not to upstage Neil Armstrong and his "one giant leap". All have wonderful stories to share.

They witnessed first-hand the extraordinary developments in British broadcasting during that decade: the transition from fuzzy live television to high-quality productions; the advent of BBC2 and then colour; the shake-up of the old wireless networks that made way for Radios 1, 2, 3 and 4…

The 1960s saw sweeping changes in British society, as relative restraint and the lingering effect of postwar austerity ceded to something altogether more permissive and vibrant – and it was all reflected in the pages of *Radio Times*, as the magazine itself became more colourful and experimental with the passing years.

One of the joys of producing *Radio Times: The Sixties* has been sifting through our archive, unearthing forgotten treasures – fascinating articles written by David Attenborough and Joe Orton, never-before-printed shots of *Z Cars* being filmed 60 years ago, and colour images from the black-and-white classics. We chanced upon two bulging photo folders for *The Forsyte Saga* and, shortly before completion, a set of precious negatives from the long-lost first series of *The Liver Birds* starring Pauline Collins.

This bounty is largely down to the efforts of one man – our staff photographer Don Smith (left). Name any programme, any 1960s icon from Dusty Springfield to the Daleks, and Don captured them on film. He was on set for nearly every *Steptoe* and *Likely Lads*. He caught Pete and Dud, Dr Finlay and Alf Garnett in their prime. Long after his retirement, he would still visit our offices each week and was a font of priceless anecdotes. Don died earlier this year aged 89. We miss our dear friend and dedicate this publication to his memory.

The 1960s? Don Smith was *everywhere* – and he could recount every detail.

OPEN THE BOX

Clockwise from above: Zebedee from *The Magic Roundabout;* the Beatles on Saturday-night TV in 1963; *The Forsyte Saga's* Kenneth More, Nyree Dawn Porter and Eric Porter; an *RT* illustration for the 1968 *Doctor Who* story, *The Web of Fear;* a rare *RT* photo of Wendy Richard in *The Newcomers* (1967), with June Bland and Robert Brown playing her parents; and (centre) Dusty Springfield and Warren Mitchell (as Alf Garnett) on the *RT* cover

Left: Don Smith with his 1966 *RT* Dalek cover, photographed by Patrick Mulkern in 2016

RADIO TIMES December 5, 1963

DECEMBER 7 — BBC tv SATURDAY

Paul McCartney — YEH! George Harrison — YEH! Ringo Starr — YEH! John Lennon

Hear them talking as the panel in *Juke Box Jury* at 6.5
IT'S THE BEATLES
Hear them singing in their own *show* at 8.10

Radio Times (Incorporating World-Radio) August 10, 1967. Vol. 176: No. 2283.

Radio Times

SIXPENCE

AUGUST 12–18

LONDON AND SOUTH-EAST

BBC-1 tv BBC-2

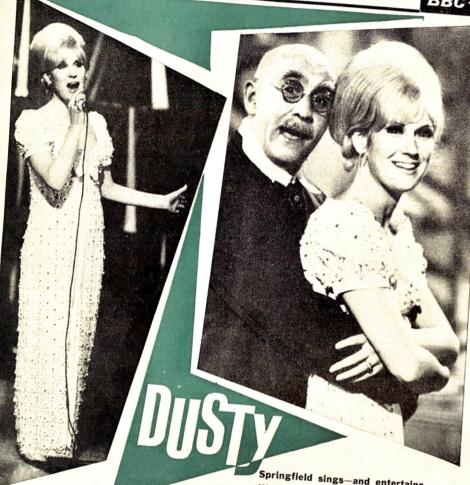

DUSTY

Springfield sings—and entertains Warren Mitchell—in her own show on Tuesday, BBC-1 (see page 23)

5

TELEVISION BBC AND SOUND
RADIO TIMES
PRICE FOURPENCE

JUNE 26—JULY 2

Radio Times (Incorporating World-Radio) June 24, 1960. Vol. 147: No. 1911.

FIRST NIGHT

OPENING OF THE BBC TELEVISION CENTRE

1960

RADIO TIMES — June 24, 1960

Opening the New BBC Television Centre

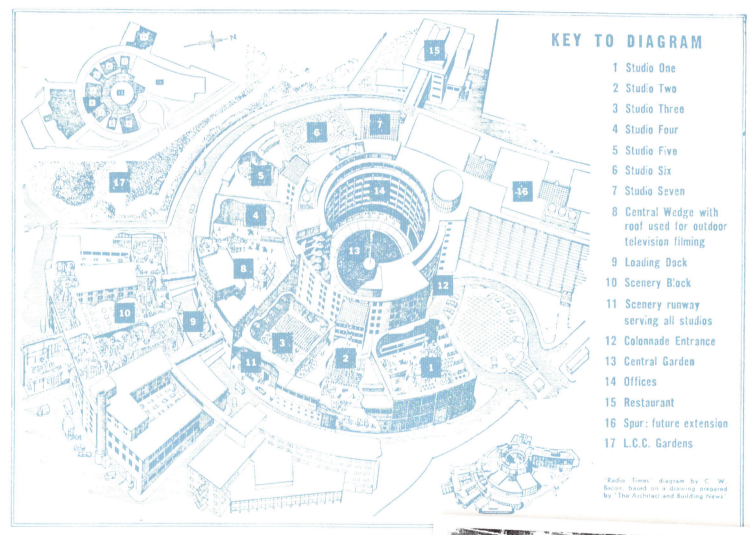

KEY TO DIAGRAM

1. Studio One
2. Studio Two
3. Studio Three
4. Studio Four
5. Studio Five
6. Studio Six
7. Studio Seven
8. Central Wedge with roof used for outdoor television filming
9. Loading Dock
10. Scenery Block
11. Scenery runway serving all studios
12. Colonnade Entrance
13. Central Garden
14. Offices
15. Restaurant
16. Spur: future extension
17. L.C.C. Gardens

'Radio Times' diagram by C. W. Bacon, based on a drawing prepared by 'The Architect and Building News'.

'It was a magical time'

By the start of the 1960s, television had emerged as a vital mass medium. One of the key BBC players at that time was Canadian-born producer/director **Alvin Rakoff**. Looking back in 2022, he tells *Radio Times*, "Television was really grabbing the audiences and having a huge effect on life in this country." However, after years of struggling to make programmes in antiquated studios such as Lime Grove ("It was held together with pieces of string"), the BBC realised a fit-for-purpose production base was essential.

On 29 June 1960, the sparkling new Television Centre in west London was officially opened with a live variety show starring magician David Nixon and comedy legends Richard Hearne (in character as Mr Pastry) and Arthur Askey. *RT* pictured them on the cover (opposite page) and provided a diagram drawn by Cecil W Bacon (above). "It was a magical, exciting time," says Rakoff. "I can't tell you how much of a relief it was when Television Centre opened – a great joy. Of course, a number of us felt that we'd built it."

TC3 Studio Three was the first to open

Radio Times
The Sixties 1960

MAIGRET

STARRING

Rupert Davies

📺 **A CRIME SERIES DRAMATISED FROM THE NOVELS OF GEORGES SIMENON**
8.45

THERE are not many people today who have not at some time or other come across the work of **Georges Simenon**: or who, having made the discovery, have not yet heard of **Inspector Maigret**. The two are now virtually inseparable. For Simenon has, since the age of twenty-five, written sixty or seventy Maigret stories, each one of which has been a best-seller. His work has been translated into some twenty-five languages and today Maigret is as famous in France, and elsewhere, as any detective to emerge from the pages of fiction in the past fifty years.

His success is not surprising. For the character of Maigret, the large, benign, shrewd, understanding, intolerant, ruthless, gentle and modest pipe-smoking detective is a man Simenon has come to know as intimately as himself, and with whom he himself can be closely identified. To know and understand Maigret, therefore, it is helpful first to take a look at the man who has brought him to life.

Georges Simenon lives near Lausanne in a lovely old château—as viewers will well remember from the filmed interview he gave to Huw Wheldon in *Monitor* last year. He is a most lively and charming person and obviously a great observer of life and character. The house is run in a highly efficient way by Mme Simenon. They do not go out a lot, but prefer to entertain in their own home, enjoying the peace and quiet of the country.

Simenon is an inveterate pipe-smoker and is seldom seen without a pipe in his mouth. He has scores of them, and a row of tobacco jars from which he mixes his particular brand. His wife cleans his pipes—about fifteen a week—and often buys them for him.

Maigret is only a small part of Simenon's work. He is a prolific writer. In fact, nowadays, writing Maigret is used as a form of relaxation which nevertheless begins at six in the morning, and ends, as far as the actual writing is concerned, at nine a.m. Three hours—and in eight days the book is finished.

The impact which Maigret has made in France has been tremendous, and has been largely responsible for a change in public opinion towards the French police. Until his appearance the police, in fiction at any rate, were presented with little sympathy and understanding. Maigret has done much to change all this and to present them in a truer light.

And now Maigret comes to BBC television in a new series of crime stories dramatised from Simenon's novels, and produced as plays by the Drama Department, with one of TV's most versatile and talented actors, **Rupert Davies**, as Maigret—a piece of casting which the Simenons agreed could not be bettered. When, in fact, Davies visited Monsieur and Madame Simenon early this year to discuss the series, he was presented with a copy of one of Simenon's books in which the author had written 'At last I have found the perfect Maigret.'

What makes this rather large, and sometimes slow-moving detective so different? In the first place he is essentially a man of sympathy. With a brilliant insight into human nature, he is nevertheless often fallible. He possesses, as Simenon himself says, the approach to crime of a really first-class G.P. His methods, too, are different from those of the usual police inspector. He much prefers calling on the person to be interviewed or interrogated to having him brought to his office. He goes, he looks, he smells, touches, senses, gets the feeling of the situation and the people he has to deal with. As a result he becomes inevitably involved in action, suspense, danger, laughter—and he sees it all with the eyes of a great humanitarian.

With this new series, which will be running for many weeks to come, the BBC has adopted a new principle. These *Maigret* productions are not films—although occasional film inserts are made as in any drama production—but recordings of performances in the television studios. Although they have been made specifically for the home market, they are also available for sale to countries abroad, and have already attracted considerable attention in America.

In overall charge, as Executive Producer, is **Andrew Osborn**, well known as both an actor and producer, with **Giles Cooper** as his script editor throughout the series. Some remarkably effective music has been specially composed by **Ron Grainer**, and for each episode a particularly strong cast has been assembled.

Playing the part of Lucas, Maigret's regular assistant, is **Ewen Solon**, while **Helen Shingler** appears as his wife. In the first exciting episode you can see tonight, *Murder in Montmartre*, you will find **Freda Jackson** and **April Olrich** in two of the principal roles.

The BBC has secured the rights to produce Maigret against world competition. Its success in obtaining the rights rested on one single fact. Simenon *wanted* the BBC to make the plays. The quality of the BBC's work impressed him and left him in little doubt as to who should produce his Maigret.

Helen Shingler as Mme. Maigret

8

Radio Times
The Sixties 1960

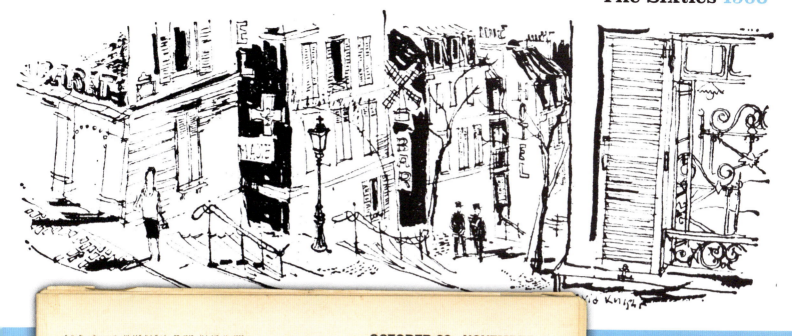

FIRST CASE
Rupert Davies, photographed by *RT*'s Don Smith at the BBC's Lime Grove Studios on 14 June 1960. The sketches of Montmartre on the cover and feature (above) were drawn by David Knight

Perfect casting

"At last I have found the perfect Maigret," wrote Georges Simenon, the French detective's creator, on meeting Rupert Davies in 1960. Reassuring praise for the seasoned English actor who was about to embark on the role that would define his career.

Although the first few editions were made at Lime Grove and Riverside Studios in London, from its seventh episode *Maigret* was the first major drama series to benefit from advanced facilities at the new BBC Television Centre. By the standards of the day, *Maigret* was a big-budget, high-quality concern – with allowance for ample filming in Paris and other parts of France. During the initial shoot in Montmartre, Davies posed for a pavement scissor-artist who produced a paper silhouette of Maigret with hat and pipe – soon adopted as an emblem for the series (opposite page).

The cast was rounded out by New Zealand-born Ewen Solon as Sergeant Lucas and Helen Shingler (mother of actors Murray and Anthony Head) as Madame Maigret.

Maigret was a huge hit in the UK and overseas, running to 52 episodes across four series. Unlike a lot of drama of that period, the entire series has been preserved in the BBC archive, and it was released as a DVD box set in 2021.

9

Radio Times
The Sixties 1960

RUPERT DAVIES

The actor who is for millions of viewers Inspector...

MAIGRET

 9.25

Leaving Television Centre one recent afternoon **Rupert Davies** was pounced on by two small boys waving pieces of paper. As he walked away after giving them his autograph, he heard one complaining bitterly: 'Here, look at this—I thought you said he was Maigret?'

Rupert sympathised with their confusion. When he first met **Georges Simenon**, the novelist told him he was the very personification of Maigret. Now, after eighteen months of virtually non-stop rehearsing, filming, and recording of twenty-four plays, TV's Maigret sometimes has to remind himself that he is Rupert Davies, actor—who in pre-Maigret days played everything from Shakespeare to Brecht and appeared in over a hundred radio and TV programmes, ranging from *Mrs. Dale's Diary* to *Monitor*.

But to the world at large, that thickset pipe-smoking figure *is* Maigret. Filming outside the Palais de Justice in Paris, Rupert was greeted by a police inspector who commiserated with him on the interference he has to put up with from the magistrate Comeliau. 'I know what it's like,' said the inspector. 'I have just the same trouble myself.' And flying back to London, he met a Q.C. who invited him to visit the Law Courts 'to see the British way of doing things.'

Mail regularly arrives at Television Centre addressed to Inspector Maigret—letters asking for advice, gifts of pipes, pouches, and tobacco. 'People must think I chew up two pipes an episode,' says Rupert, 'although I've only got through one since the series started. I'm often asked to send a few pipes to be auctioned for charity, and one autograph-hunter was quite offended when I wouldn't part with my briar.'

Wherever he goes, Maigret-Davies is recognised. Taking a couple of days off in Devon last August, he was so often stopped by holiday-makers that he began to appreciate the feelings of a hunted crook. 'The maddening thing is that on the few occasions when I would *like* to be recognised, because it could be useful—getting a restaurant table, perhaps, or cashing a cheque—it always turns out that the chap I want to impress doesn't watch TV...'

PETER BROWNE

EVIDENCE ON FILE

The *Radio Times* archive has preserved a large folder of photographs taken by Don Smith and Joan Williams – as well as the Maigret silhouette often used to illustrate articles. The images (left) are from the very first episode in 1960, while (below) Rupert Davies was photographed in colour when the inspector made a comeback in 1969 for *Play of the Month*

Radio Times
The Sixties 1960

Captain Pugwash is Back!

CAPTAIN PUGWASH and his pirates pop into view again on Sunday. Pugwash began his cartoon adventures in television in 1957, so you have probably come to know already what a bungler he is. What can you make of a man who puts gunpowder in the teapot, and mistakes a big enemy ship for a small one because he has got his telescope back to front?

Luckily for him and his muddle-headed men, their worst enemy, Cut-Throat Jake, is even more stupid. And Jake's pirates are so dense they make Pugwash's crew seem almost clever. Actually, the only bright one on Pugwash's ship, the *Black Pig*, is Tom the Cabin Boy. He tries to keep the crew on their toes.

Pugwash and his friends and foes sprang to life some years ago in the mind of artist John Ryan. He began them as still pictures, but now, in television, they go into action. Arms wave, eyes roll, mouths snap open and shut, and swords flash and guns belch smoke. There's no need for printed words, though, because Peter Hawkins, that man of many voices, makes the pirates talk.

Each adventure is told in about fifty separate pictures. Having thought of the plot, John Ryan sketches the outlines on sheets of cardboard, with separate drawings of arms and legs and anything else that has to move. Then one of his assistants, Colin Garland, does the painting and cutting out, and Hazel Martingell afterwards fits everything together for the animation.

Before the long string of cartoons go to the studios for telerecording, John Ryan gets a lot of advice from his children. Marianne, aged eight, and Christopher, five, are experts. After all, they've lived with the Pugwash crowd a long time now.

ERNEST THOMSON

Look out for a new strip cartoon about Captain Pugwash by John Ryan beginning in the next Junior Radio Times.

AHOY THERE!

Captain Pugwash began life in the 1950s as a cartoon in the children's comic *Eagle* – before graduating to a BBC TV series and a regular strip in *Radio Times*, drawn by his creator, John Ryan. Peter Hawkins, who provided voices for the pirate captain and his crew on TV, also voiced Bill and Ben in *The Flowerpot Men* and, later, *Doctor Who's* Daleks and Cybermen

PUGWASH AHOY!
By JOHN RYAN

PAUSE FOR THOUGHT

In February 1960, BBC Radio was embracing the new wave of playwrights making names for themselves in British theatreland. The distinguished critic Kenneth A Hurren evidently had more faith in Arnold Wesker and his "widely praised" *Roots* (which starred Joan Plowright) than Harold Pinter and the "obscure horrors" promised by *A Night Out* (starring Barry Foster)

RADIO DRAMA
By KENNETH A. HURREN

Two Promising Young Playwrights

THE British theatre, over which touching but premature requiems are intoned from time to time, enters the 1960s more richly endowed with gifted young dramatists than at any other single period of its history. They may not all fulfil their initial promise. But John Osborne, Arnold Wesker, John Arden, Brendan Behan, John Mortimer, Willis Hall, Peter Shaffer—perhaps also J. P. Donleavy and Harold Pinter—are men whose talents guarantee that the immediate future of our drama will be vibrant, exciting, stimulating, and essentially of our own time. Two of them are represented in this week's radio drama: Arnold Wesker by *Roots*, one of the most widely praised plays of 1959 (Monday, Home), and Harold Pinter by a piece written specially for this medium, *A Night Out* (Tuesday, Third).

* * *

Harold Pinter's approach to drama is considerably less conventional than Mr. Wesker's and it is still a controversial question whether he has, in fact, a serious and worthy contribution to make to the playhouse. His only full-length play so far produced was a commercial disaster, but that is not necessarily relevant in considering the merits of a new writer. There are critics who exalt him above all his fellows.

A Night Out affords listeners an opportunity to take sides, at least tentatively, for this strange account of a night in the life of a young man possessively dominated by his mother contains in abundance the odd humours and obscure horrors that typify Mr. Pinter's dramatic world.

ARNOLD WESKER (*Roots*)   HAROLD PINTER (*A Night Out*)

David Attenborough

'I THINK,' said David Attenborough, looking out of the window at a dull grey afternoon in London, 'I must be one of the luckiest people I know. After all, who else is in a position to open an atlas, pinpoint some remote part of the world, say "I'd like to go there for a few months," and receive the permission and the blessing of his employers?'

Putting it like that, and characteristically understating his own part in organising and producing some of the most enchanting, exciting, and illuminating travel programmes that have ever been shown on television, David Attenborough invests his job with an atmosphere of simple adventure that belongs to the pages of schoolboy fiction. But as anyone who has seen his previous *Zoo Quests* and who has joined him on his current journey to the South Seas will know, these programmes stem from the imagination not of a fiction writer, but of a man of science, whose education as a zoologist, whose training as a television producer, and whose appreciation of both the beautiful and the incongruous have been happily welded together inside a sympathetic and enthusiastic personality.

Unlike that of his distinguished actor-brother Richard, David's emergence and success as a 'performer' was unintentional. When the late Jack Lester, with whom he collaborated in the first *Zoo Quest* to West Africa, fell ill in the middle of the series, David took over in the studio and immediately endeared himself to viewers with his friendly and understanding handling of the animals they had brought back. Lester recovered sufficiently to undertake another journey—this time to British Guiana—but becoming ill on the trip, he returned to Britain and David continued alone.

With *The People of Paradise* (Thursday) now occupying his working weeks, he has not had a chance to formulate a plan for his next series. But in the coming months he will undoubtedly be opening that atlas again, taking out his pin, and contemplating another difficult and often dangerous assignment which most other people consider themselves lucky to be able to enjoy in the comfort of their homes. ROWAN AYERS

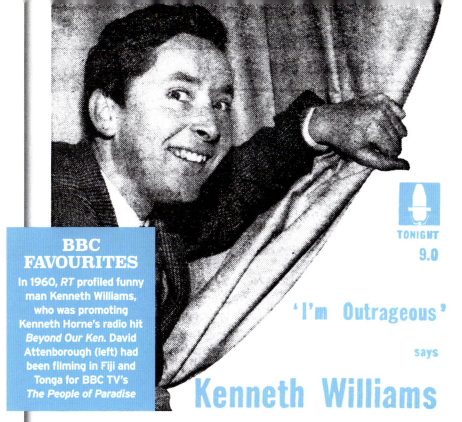

BBC FAVOURITES
In 1960, *RT* profiled funny man Kenneth Williams, who was promoting Kenneth Horne's radio hit *Beyond Our Ken*. David Attenborough (left) had been filming in Fiji and Tonga for BBC TV's *The People of Paradise*

TONIGHT 9.0

'I'm Outrageous' says Kenneth Williams

'But not by choice'—he is quick to add with a twitch of his nose and that sad, owlish smile which, by some miracle, he manages to plant across the microphone as the 'refained' Rodney to Hugh Paddick's Charles in *Beyond Our Ken*.

The 'outrages' began about six years ago when this London-born Welshman, then twenty-eight, was cast as an awful, bespectacled twelve-year-old in the Sandy Wilson play, *The Buccaneer*. 'This reputation has clung to me ever since,' he says. 'All through the *Carry On* films. In *Carry On Nurse* I was the awful patient cheeking the matron. In *Carry On Constable* I was the rude, crude policeman. It'll be the same in my next picture, *Carry On Regardless*—an outrageous intellectual.'

Intellectual—though not outrageously so—he certainly is in real life. He has a passion for reading, mainly biography and history, a devotion to gothic calligraphy and illuminated manscripts, a deep love for the music of Schumann. (He has a record-player in his bachelor flat near Marble Arch, but no radio or television.)

And how did this slender young printer find himself in show business? In Bolt Court, off London's Fleet Street, he was learning lithography when the Army took him, at eighteen, to India. By a freak of fortune he was transferred from the Royal Engineers to Combined Services Entertainment, touring Malaya and Burma and fetching up at the Victoria Theatre, Singapore. Here, in his rawness, he perpetrated on Stanley Baxter (they were put on as a double act) the most outrageous 'fluff' in the history of modern drama. Kenneth explains. 'Stanley was supposed to say—"They're wonderfully honest in Cairo. I left my watch on a lamp-post. When I went back a year later it was still there." My comeback should have been, "What, the watch?" And his: "No, the lamp-post." Instead, I said—"What, the lamp-post?"'

Nevertheless, Kenneth decided to carry on. Home again in 'civvies,' he got himself into repertory companies all over the country. In 1950 he achieved his peak, as he thought then, as the tragic young Hugo in Sartre's *Crime Passionel* with Clifford Evans's company at Swansea. 'That's still my favourite serious role. Even more so than my Dauphin with Siobhan McKenna in *St. Joan*.'

Kenneth Williams is essentially a character actor. He has played Shakespeare and Sheridan, was Slightly in *Peter Pan* with Brenda Bruce, and took the West End lead in *Share My Lettuce*. Listeners first got to know him well in *Hancock's Half-Hour*.

Taut and sensitive, he loves the theatre and a living audience. 'That's where you score with comedy and farce over tragedy,' he says. 'The comeback is immediate. You can "play" your audience, too, and as every one is different, that makes it still more exciting.'

It is odd, perhaps, that one so susceptible to crowd stimulus, and the clash and glare of the theatre, should set so much store by personal privacy—'my flat is my bachelor island.' He does his own cooking and cleaning. Mostly the cooking is coffee only—his breakfast. All day he is out rehearsing or filming.

I came back to the question everyone asks. 'How do you manage to look so young?' The nose gave a mischievous twitch. 'No responsibilities—absolutely none. Isn't it outrageous?' ERNEST THOMSON

JUNE 23 **FRIDAY**

MAY 20—26

Radio Times (Incorporating World-Radio) May 18, 1961. Vol. 151: No. 1958.

BBC RADIO TIMES
tv and SOUND

5D

HANCOCK
FRIDAY: TELEVISION

1961

May 18, 1961   RADIO TIMES

HE'S BACK
HE'S BACK
HE'S BACK
HANCOCK

FRIDAY

■ 8.0 'AH yes,' sighed the one-time squire of East Cheam, as we discussed his new series with him in the cultured atmosphere of his Earls Court bed-sitter, 'it's good-bye to all that black homburg hat and astrakhan collar rubbish. Knowledge and self-advancement are the things—.' This was definitely the rebel speaking, kicking against society, the Establishment, and all the irritating restrictions imposed upon those men who are prepared to use their initiative. 'Their loaf, mate' were his actual words, but then Hancock was ever a pioneer of the vernacular. 'That's right,' said Tony, reaching for a dictionary. 'Mountain railways and all that . . .'

As you can see from our cover this week, the lad is not only back, but has acquired, since his adventures in film-land, a kind of confident gloss that will doubtless serve him in good stead for the next six weeks.

For his first show tonight he is on his own for the whole twenty-five minutes. Yes, twenty-five minutes ('You'll never be able to call it "'Ancock's Arf-hour" again, mate')—and if you think it will be difficult for him to find enough to do and say to hold your interest, we should perhaps point out that those two inseparables **Ray Galton** and **Alan Simpson**, who have been writing BBC shows for Hancock since 1954, admitted that they have already had to cut out nearly twenty minutes of script to get the programme down to length.

'For this series,' they told us, 'we're not developing any elaborate plots—just creating situations and giving Tony the chance to sort things out—his way. Next week, for instance, he gets stuck in a lift, and the following week he turns to amateur radio!'

This is the seventh series of Hancock shows to be put on by BBC Television, and the producer is once again **Duncan Wood**. 'When it's over,' said Tony, 'I'm off to America for a month to go round with my film—making personal appearances. And one place I'm determined to visit, even if it is hell, is Las Vegas.'

MULTIPLE TONYS

In 1961, after six radio series and seven on TV, comedy star Tony Hancock was leaving the BBC. *RT*'s **Don Smith** recalled in 2014, "Several years ago I had a call from a man in the Midlands who runs the Tony Hancock Appreciation Society. He said that, according to their records, I'd photographed Hancock for six *Radio Times* covers. I never realised that.

"Towards the end of his life Tony was drinking heavily, but I never had any trouble with him. You have to know how far you can go and when to lay off. It can be irritating when photographers ask for 'just one more'. You don't want to bore your subject to death. I've never been very creative, but I did shine in seizing the moment – which is difficult at times."

JUNE 23

BBC tv

Radio Times
The Sixties 1961

AN ARMFUL
RT's Don Smith was on set to capture many classic *Hancock* TV episodes, including *The Blood Donor* on 2 June 1961. Tony Hancock is pictured below with co-stars Frank Thornton and June Whitfield

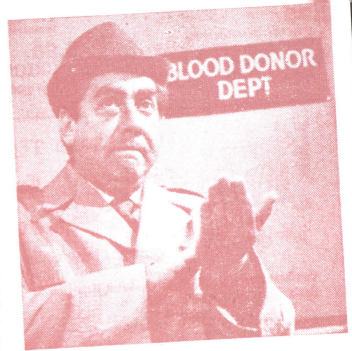

★ **Hancock** sets a good example tonight by becoming a blood-donor. Assisting in the operation are Patrick Cargill as a doctor, and June Whitfield as a nurse.

at 8.0

ON YOUR SCREENS TONIGHT

Take your pick. There's something for everyone on BBC Television tonight. Music, drama, comedy, travel, you'll find them all there . . .

16

PHOTOGRAPH BY DON SMITH

Radio Times
The Sixties 1961

MAYDAY!
In May 1961, Don Smith photographed Hancock in another popular edition, *The Radio Ham*

Before Bond

Mere months before being cast as James Bond in *Dr No*, Sean Connery graced the *RT* cover as Alexander the Great in *Adventure Story*, an adaptation of a Terence Rattigan stage play.

Director **Alvin Rakoff** had been instrumental in Connery's gradual rise to fame in the 1950s. "Sean was an extra, a walk-on, and occasionally I'd give him a line or two as most producer/directors did," Rakoff tells *RT* in 2022. "But, in 1957, I gave him his first leading role as a boxer in *Requiem for a Heavyweight*, an American play by Rod Serling. The star, Jack Palance, pulled out and I spent the weekend desperately looking for someone else.

"The lady playing the lead in it [Jacqueline Hill], who became my first wife shortly afterwards, said, 'Have you seen Sean?' And I said, 'Don't be silly. You can't understand a word he says. He mumbles.' Then she said, 'The ladies would like it. Think about it.' So I auditioned Sean and by the Sunday night decided to give it to him."

Connery was a success, and further lead TV roles soon followed. By 1961, he was under consideration to star in the first Bond movie. Rakoff was sounded out by *Dr No's* co-producer, fellow Canadian Harry Saltzman, because he'd worked with all three contenders for the part – Patrick McGoohan, Roger Moore and Sean Connery. "He asked my opinion, which was that Patrick was by far the best actor but not the easiest of people to deal with, Roger was the most affable and certainly capable, and that Sean would be the most interesting. I was delighted when I heard he'd got the part."

Of course, McGoohan made his name in ITV shows *Danger Man* and *The Prisoner*, while Moore became *The Saint* and – in the 1970s – 007.

Adventure Story

ALEXANDER the Great, on his death-bed, re-lives his turbulent life of conquest and intrigue in **Terence Rattigan's** drama, *Adventure Story*, to be televised next Monday, starring **Sean Connery** as Alexander and **Margaretta Scott** as the Queen Mother. This play was first produced at the St. James's Theatre in London in March, 1949, and had its television première on July 30, 1950.

Adventure Story is produced by Rudolph Cartier. Others in the cast are William Russell, Lyndon Brook, Alex Scott, William Devlin, Michael Brennan, Paul Stassino, Noel Hood and Bandana Das Gupta.

Radio Times
The Sixties 1961

TUESDAY

A for ANDROMEDA

8.30

BEHIND barbed wire at Thorness, a remote rocket-testing base in the Western Isles, a group of scientists led by brilliant John Fleming are working on Project *A for Andromeda*. Strange signals picked up by a powerful radio-telescope from a source millions of miles away in outer space, somewhere in the constellation Andromeda, have been interpreted by Fleming as mathematical instructions for building a huge computer—an electronic 'brain'—of fantastic complexity, and the decision has been taken at Cabinet level to go ahead and build it.

In the third episode of the serial tonight the outstanding cast which already includes **Esmond Knight, Noel Johnson, Peter Halliday, Patricia Kneale,** and **Julie Christie** will be further strengthened by the first appearance in it of **Mary Morris**, playing Professor Dawnay, a distinguished biologist who sees Project Andromeda as a heaven-sent opportunity for laboratory research. Miss Morris, like several other members of the cast, played a memorable part in the *Age of Kings* Shakespeare series, of which **Michael Hayes**, co-producer of *Andromeda*, was director.

For Julie Christie, on the other hand, the role of Christine is her first major one in television: Hayes discovered her recently at a drama school exercise.

When Julie became Susan

Following in the tradition of Nigel Kneale's three exciting *Quatermass* serials in the 1950s, *A for Andromeda* was the BBC's first major foray into science fiction in the 1960s – and it starred 21-year-old Julie Christie. Wearing a black wig (on the *RT* cover, right), she began the series as scientist Christine, who was cloned by an alien intelligence – emerging as the robotic, blonde Andromeda.

It launched Christie's career, and she was soon being offered film roles and clocked up classics such as *Billy Liar* (1963), *Darling* (above, 1965) – for which she won an Oscar – and *Doctor Zhivago* (1965).

She proved unavailable when a sequel, *The Andromeda Breakthrough,* was made in 1962, so the strange role of Andromeda was gifted to 25-year-old **Susan Hampshire** (far right). "I was actually a little bit out of my depth," Hampshire tells *RT* in 2022. "I've often done parts that other people have created first and you never feel very confident. But the cast – Peter Halliday and Mary Morris – were all very kind, encouraging me to be like a zombie." She laughs. "I did my best, is all I can say!"

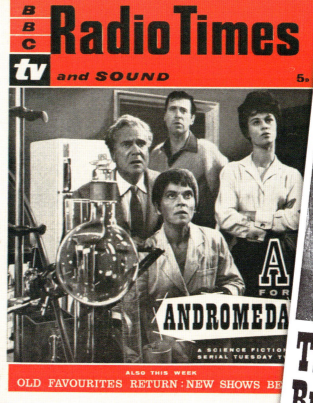

Radio Times (Incorporating World-Radio) February 1, 1962. Vol. 154: No. 1995.

FEBRUARY 3—9

BBC RADIO Times
tv and SOUND

5d

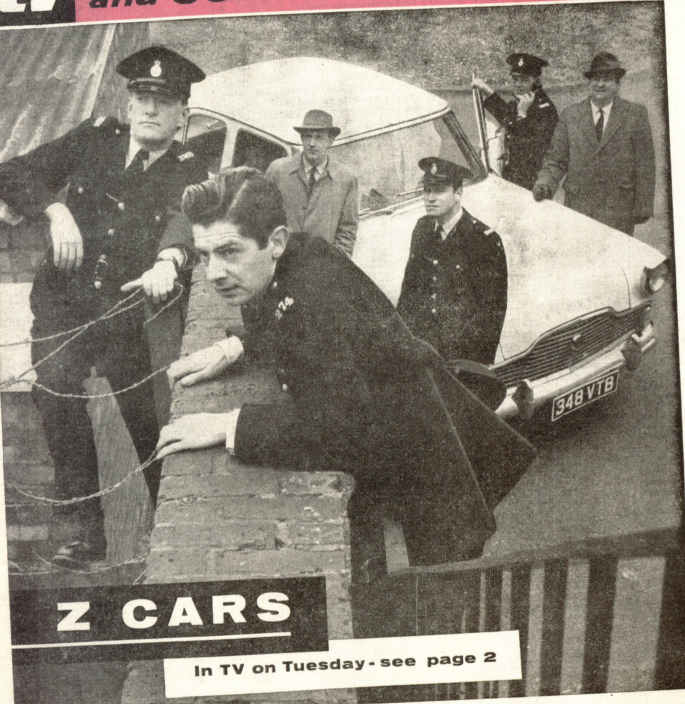

Z CARS
In TV on Tuesday - see page 2

1962

RADIO TIMES — December 28, 1961

Z CARS

They fight crime on wheels in a new series beginning tonight

Frank Windsor

Brian Blessed

Joe Brady

James Ellis

Jeremy Kemp

Stratford Johns

Z VICTOR

In contrast to the much-loved but staid *Dixon of Dock Green* (a police drama running since 1955), *Z Cars* caused a sensation in 1962 with its racy plots and fast action. Created by Troy Kennedy Martin, the series made stars of, among others, Stratford Johns, Frank Windsor, Brian Blessed and James Ellis. In December 1961, *RT*'s Don Smith photographed the early location filming — and would capture *Z Cars* throughout its 16-year run

21

RADIO TIMES   *July 19, 1962*

TUESDAY

Four young actors look back over thirty weeks as the popular Police Constables of . . .

Z cars

> **FAST WORK**
>
> In its early years, *Z Cars* was transmitted live. Exterior action and location sequences would be filmed in advance and inserted during the live broadcast. Other demanding set-ups were also shot ahead of time at Ealing Film Studios, as shown in these rare photos from 1962. Director Alvin Rakoff is circled (right), and guest star Ronald Lacey is pictured on set (bottom)

Lynch (James Ellis) and Steele (Jeremy Kemp)

Smith (Brian Blessed) and Weir (Joseph Brady)

7.55

JEREMY KEMP was having trouble with his powerful green sports car. Stuck midway across a London street, he struggled to shift an obstinate gear lever, while passers-by stopped, stared, and grinned. 'Come on, Steele, get cracking... where's your chum Lynch?...BD to Z Victor Two, have you lost your patrol car?'

It's the sort of thing that happens all the time to BBC-tv's two teams of Newtown constables. Everywhere they go they are spotted. Everyone, it seems, is a fan of *Z Cars*.

Bob Steele and Herbert Lynch, Fancy Smith and Jock Weir...off screen they are friends, too, and looking back over the series which comes off for a six-week rest next week, they agree that it has been quite an experience.

The flood of fan mail, for example. Like the letter to Jock (**Joseph Brady**) from two sisters who wrote that they never missed an episode 'but this Tuesday we have to go to a party. Will you please postpone the programme till Wednesday?' A small boy appealed to Lynch (**James Ellis**): 'Can you help me find my bike?' And a schoolgirl wrote to **Jeremy Kemp**: 'Nobody else in my class likes you, but I think you're smashing. It's always been my ambition to be a policewoman. How do I go about it?'

Then there have been the unforgettable experiences while out filming on location. James Ellis remembers vividly the scene in the first episode when he stood at a crossroads near Liverpool, directing traffic. 'Everything got into a hopeless tangle, while the real point-duty policeman stood by the roadside laughing.'

All four are amazed at the way they have become identified in so many people's minds as real policemen. Even in civilian clothes Jeremy Kemp has been stopped in the street and asked for directions. And one day while Jock and Fancy (**Brian Blessed**) were sitting in their patrol car waiting for the cameras to turn a woman rushed up and said: 'Come quickly, my house has been burgled.' When the two actors tried to explain that they were not policemen, the woman was highly indignant. 'Oh, yes, you are,' she said. 'I've seen you on television.'

Fifteen million viewers will miss those four familiar faces during their six-week absence. But for the *Z Cars* men it is their first chance in nearly eight months' non-stop work to take a break. (Two hours after next Tuesday's episode ends, Jeremy Kemp will be flying to Greece—where, he hopes, he may escape the motor-cyclists who so often tail his car, whistling the *Z Cars* theme.) But they'll be back in September for new adventures in this fantastically popular series, which—as one policeman has put it—'is as near to the truth as you can get.'

Radio Times
The Sixties 1962

'Z Cars was Pow!'

So popular was *Z Cars*, it was quickly commissioned for a second season. On 3 September 1962, *Radio Times* sent photographer Don Smith to Ealing Film Studios, where the actor James Ellis (PC Bert Lynch) was performing a scene for the first episode.

These previously unpublished images capture the production team at work, including director **Alvin Rakoff**, who is delighted to see them 60 years later. "Ah yes, the sullen young man next to the camera, cigarette in hand, is me," he tells *RT* in 2022. "To my right is my faithful floor manager Mary Ridge, who later became a director. The young man facing the camera is Ronald Lacey, who went on to a long film career, achieving Hollywood fame with Steven Spielberg. A good actor and helluva nice guy."

Z Cars followed the pattern of many TV dramas in the early 1960s, with some exterior scenes and car chases filmed in advance to be played back during the live broadcast from the studio. Rakoff recalls this process as "exciting and frightening", and reveres *Z Cars* as "a remarkable phenomenon of that era". With another, perhaps more prestigious, project on hold (a Terence Rattigan play starring Ralph Richardson and Kenneth More), Rakoff was asked to "do a *Z Cars*". He says, "I grabbed at it because I was so impressed. It was revolutionary.

"To me, there were two landmark occasions in those early days. One was the Queen's Coronation in 1953, which made millions go and buy television sets for the first time, and the other was *Z Cars*. It appealed to the masses. It did drastically grab the audiences and change them completely. *Z Cars* was a Pow! programme."

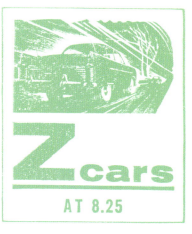

23

Radio Times
The Sixties 1962

'I was dying 1,000 deaths'

Launched on 2 January 1962, *Compact* was a twice-weekly soap set in the offices of a women's magazine and offered a glamorous alternative to ITV's *Coronation Street*. A popular show, it ran for three and a half years, but **Waris Hussein**, who directed ten of the early episodes, recalls that "*Compact* was a load of absolute drivel". He laughs, telling *RT* 60 years later, "Despite that, the cast thought very highly of themselves, while its creators, Peter Ling and Hazel Adair [who later devised ITV soap *Crossroads*], behaved as though they were the lord and lady of Television Centre."

Fresh from the BBC directors' course, Hussein truly cut his teeth on *Compact*. "The Tuesday edition was shown live, before the next was recorded 'as live' for broadcast on Thursday. I'll never forget my first episode [2 October 1962]. I'd carefully choreographed it for the four cameras in the studio, but during the live transmission Camera One broke down – so we couldn't utilise any of those shots. You can't imagine what I was going through. I felt like I was in one of those Hollywood movies where Doris Day is suddenly asked to land a passenger plane…" He had to revise his directions on the hoof for the three remaining cameras. "I got through it without them crashing into each other, but I was dying a thousand deaths by the time the end credits went up. I collapsed in the director's chair. The team had to take me to the bar and give me a strong drink."

Compact wasn't the first job at the BBC for the Indian-born director, who many years later would win a Bafta for *Edward & Mrs Simpson* (ITV, 1978). Hussein's earliest credit in *Radio Times* appeared on 2 February 1962 in the cast list of a forgotten drama, *You Can't Win 'Em All*.

"Oh yes, I played a South American freedom fighter called Cholo, rather like Che Guevara. I had to jump off fake rocks in the studio and looked incredibly butch and quite pretty. That was my first claim to fame, but of course the BBC wiped the recording. Now nobody can see my Cholo," he chuckles. Luckily, a photograph survives (below).

1962
Top: *Compact* stars Monica Evans and Ronald Allen celebrating their 50th edition
Left: Waris Hussein acting in *You Can't Win 'Em All*

A BBC-TV series which tells the inside story of a women's magazine

compact

 7.30

WHEN a talented and temperamental group of men and women work together in the hothouse atmosphere of women's journalism, there's often far more drama —and romance—behind the scenes than between the covers of their magazine. Such is the setting for *Compact*, the new serial beginning this evening and following the twice-weekly pattern which BBC-tv's *Starr & Co.* established so successfully in the past.

Compact is a new and different kind of women's magazine. A pocket-size, topical weekly, aimed at the busy woman—the brain-child of Joanne Minster (played by **Jean Harvey**), its elegant, attractive Editor. The magazine is an independent venture, in competition with the powerful publishing combines. Backed by a wealthy industrialist, its offices occupy one of the floors in the vast London headquarters of his world-wide enterprises.

In this evening's first episode of the serial, the first issue of *Compact* has just hit the bookstalls. The editorial team have been working together for six months planning the magazine, and now they face the moment of truth: how will the public react?

The long and short of it: Sheila Hancock, Esma Cannon, and Miriam Karlin

FRIDAY

THE RAG TRADE

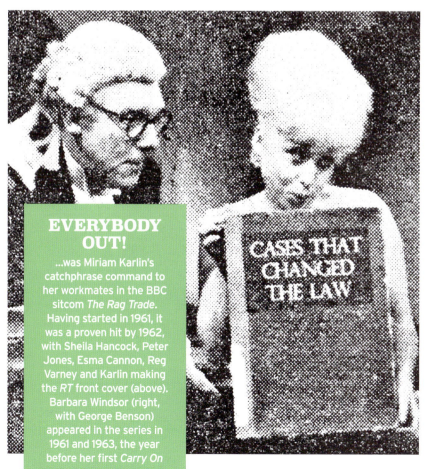

EVERYBODY OUT!

...was Miriam Karlin's catchphrase command to her workmates in the BBC sitcom *The Rag Trade*. Having started in 1961, it was a proven hit by 1962, with Sheila Hancock, Peter Jones, Esma Cannon, Reg Varney and Karlin making the *RT* front cover (above). Barbara Windsor (right, with George Benson) appeared in the series in 1961 and 1963, the year before her first *Carry On*

7.30 ONE recent Friday morning Paddy, Lily, and Carole of *The Rag Trade* sat side-by-side on a bench in a dusty Fulham rehearsal hall and considered the effect on their lives of appearing in one of the most popular comedy series ever televised.

'You can't get away from it,' said **Miriam** (**Paddy**) **Karlin**. 'Even on holiday in Majorca, people came up to me and said: " Where's your whistle, love? "'

' I've lost count,' said **Esma** (**Lily**) **Cannon**, ' of the number of times people have stopped me in the street and said: " You're just like my aunt." Apparently there's a Lil in every family.'

' It gets embarrassing,' said **Sheila** (**Carole**) **Hancock**, ' when you're riding on an underground train and some bright spark yells " Everybody out! "'

The on-screen antics of the three thorns in the flesh of Fenner Fashions are followed every week by an audience of some fourteen and a half million viewers—and the large fan-mail they receive indicates how firmly the characters they play have become established.

Said Miriam: ' There was a viewer who wrote to me " from one seamstress to another," giving me her measurements and asking for a spare dressmaker's dummy.'

Said Esma : ' A handsome pokerwork plaque arrived the other day inscribed " Little but Good." '

Said Sheila, who is currently in a London revue: ' Nearly every evening someone in the audience blows a whistle.'

And all three revealed a trade secret which, when you consider the staff of Fenner Fashions, is hardly surprising: since *The Rag Trade* series began the actual output from the sewing-machines in Studio Four at the BBC's Television Centre has been three somewhat cock-eyed cushion covers.

Radio Times
The Sixties 1962

Harry H. Corbett as Harold and Wilfrid Brambell as Albert

STEPTOE AND SON

8.45

Several years ago, in a Shepherd's Bush eel-and-pie shop, scriptwriters **Alan Simpson** and **Ray Galton** became intrigued by the strange slang that two men sitting nearby were using. They were, it turned out, junk dealers, and Alan and Ray made a note to do something about such characters some day.

They finally did it last January in their *Comedy Playhouse* series, with 'The Offer'—the saga of Albert and Harold Steptoe and their junkyard. So enthusiastic was the play's reception from viewers and critics that the authors were asked to build a series of programmes round the same pair.

Steptoe and Son begins tonight with a repeat showing of 'The Offer,' and for the next five Thursdays we shall be following the fortunes of the Steptoes. **Wilfrid Brambell** plays artful old Albert, while **Harry H. Corbett** is his son Harold, the frustrated junkman with a yearning for finer things.

Ron Grainer, who wrote all the music for *Comedy Playhouse*, performs the same service for *Steptoe and Son*. His catchy theme for 'The Offer,' called 'Old Ned,' becomes the signature tune of the new series.

When producer **Duncan Wood** went looking for a suitable junkyard in which to film exterior scenes, he found it just round the corner from the BBC's Television Centre in London. Sections of the yard have been duplicated in the studio.

RAG AND BONE

Hancock writers Ray Galton and Alan Simpson had another ace sitcom up their sleeves with *Steptoe and Son*. Launching under the *Comedy Playhouse* banner on 5 January 1962, it soon led to a series that summer and made stars of Wilfrid Brambell and Harry H Corbett as the father-and-son scrap merchants. As well as eight series between 1962 and 1974, *Steptoe and Son* was adapted for radio and spawned two films

Comedy Playhouse: THE OFFER

Albert Steptoe's son, Harold, finds it difficult when he tries to break away from his father's rag-and-bone business

★ **AT 8.45**

LIKE FATHER…?

Radio Times photographer Don Smith recalled in 2014, "I got on well with Wilfrid Brambell and Harry H Corbett, although I believe they ended up hating each other. I photographed them hundreds of times, for every episode"

Radio Times
The Sixties 1962

Harry H. Corbett AS HAROLD IN **STEPTOE AND SON**

8.45

CONSIDER Harold Steptoe... a frustrated junk dealer trapped by his own limitations and a cunning old father in a job he hates; a man full of vague ambition for a more rewarding life which always seems to be just out of reach. How do you see him—as a figure of fun, or a figure of tragedy?

Harry H. Corbett, who plays Harold in *Steptoe and Son*, sees him as a kind of latter-day Walter Mitty—'He has his dreams all day, and so do we; it's in all of us and we never lose it. And he's a man in the grip of that terrifying dilemma—how long do you stand by your duties and let life slip away from you?

'There are so many people in the same situation. A lot is written about the problems of teenagers and old folk, but the thirties have their troubles, too, and to me *Steptoe* is basically an exploration of this theme. It's a marriage of light entertainment and drama, it's tragi-comedy—and that's life.'

The analysis is characteristic of Corbett, an accomplished actor who has been seen in many TV plays (his last for BBC-tv was *A Matter of Conscience*) and has for ten years been closely associated with that home of controversial stage productions, London's Theatre Workshop.

In *Steptoe*, he is in his element: 'To get the chance of building a character like Harold in *The Offer* was wonderful—to be able to develop this character for a further five episodes is paradise for an actor.' He is developing it to such good purpose that while wandering down a corridor in Television Centre during a break in rehearsals the other day, he was spotted as a suspicious and un-BBC-like type, and nearly thrown out.

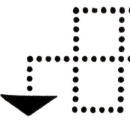

POINTS FROM THE POST

...and Son

I'VE often enjoyed a programme but never before put pen to paper in order to say so.

I would, however, like to show my appreciation of the new series of *Steptoe and Son* (BBC-tv, Thursdays). It is a tonic—I've not laughed so much for a long time, and yet there is always a touch of pathos.

Wilfrid Brambell and Harry H. Corbett are wonderful, and the incidental music perfect.

Poor Harold tries so hard to be a 'gent,' but never quite makes it. I'm greatly looking forward to the next episode in a series in which I am sure the BBC has a winner.—(Mrs.) S. Robson, Barrow-in-Furness.

Funniest Ever

I THOROUGHLY agree with your correspondent Mrs. S. Robson. *Steptoe and Son* is the funniest programme I have ever seen on television.

But I see with great disappointment that the present series will end on July 12. I do hope this programme will make a quick return to our screens.

Harry H. Corbett and Wilfrid Brambell are marvellous.—S. Bishop, Southend-on-Sea.

There will be a new series of Steptoe and Son in the winter.—Editor.

Poor Harold!

I FOUND the recently repeated series of *Steptoe and Son* absolutely heart-breaking—especially the last episode, which upset me so much that I had to keep going out of the room for short intervals because I couldn't stand it.

If there is going to be another series I suggest to the writers that dear, good, kind Harold, who tries so hard to better himself, gets his own way just occasionally.

Please give him a girl friend, and marry him off in the last episode to someone who can keep that selfish, sly old man in his place.—(Miss) Margaret Wareing, Aberystwyth.

ANY OLD IRON

In 1965, Wilfrid Brambell and Harry H Corbett gamely posed for this *RT* cover shoot, promoting their fourth series together. It would be their last for five years. They returned to BBC1 in colour in 1970

 **THURSDAY**

WILFRID BRAMBELL who is . . .

. . . ALBERT of Steptoe and Son

📺 8.45   Most of the outdoor scenes for *Steptoe and Son* are filmed in a junkyard in Shepherds Bush, London, just around the corner from the BBC's Television Centre. It was there one morning recently that **Wilfrid Brambell**, who plays old Albert Steptoe, was waiting for the signal to lead his horse and cart in front of the cameras when a junk dealer standing nearby asked: 'Are they using you, mate?'

'I admitted that they were,' Brambell recalls, 'and with great compassion in his eyes he looked at me and my poor knacker-worthy horse and said encouragingly: "Oh, well, they'll probably give you a few bob."'

Which helps to explain why whenever a part comes up for a particularly scruffy old character, producers think of Brambell —who is in fact spruce and agile and barely fifty.

He first took a flying leap into his dotage some seven years ago in the television version of *1984*, in which he was cast as an octogenarian—so successfully that he soon found himself doddering again in *Quatermass*, and has since appeared in elderly parts ('it gets easier every year,' he says cheerfully) in numerous films and TV plays. He has been seen recently as John Mills's father in *Flame in the Streets* and as a disreputable fisherman in the BBC-tv production of *The Long Memory*; and he has just finished filming as 'a crazy, hairy old maniac' in Walt Disney's *The Castaways*.

'Today,' says Brambell, 'it takes me longer to look fifty than it does to look eighty. I don't use make-up; I just stop shaving for a few days, they dirty me down a bit, and that's it.'

The one disadvantage of ageing so easily: 'Where other actors get film parts that take them on location to glamorous places like Bermuda and Tahiti, my broken-down characters always seem to end up somewhere like Shepherds Bush or the Elephant and Castle!'

Radio Times
The Sixties 1962

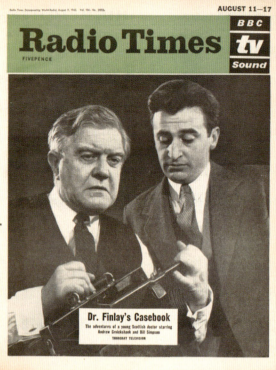

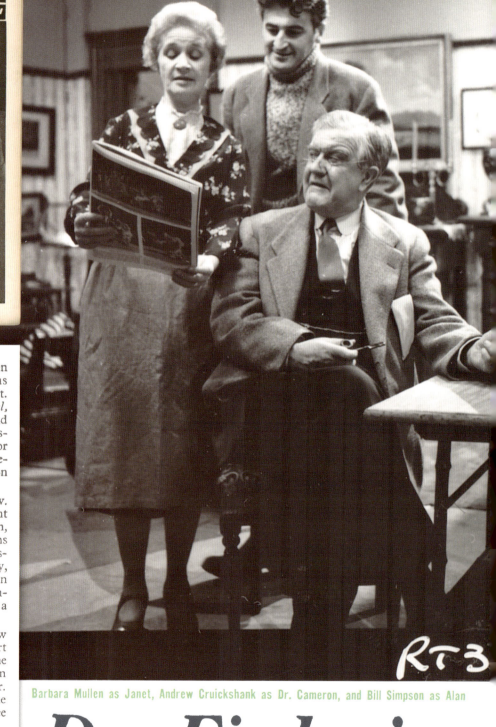

Barbara Mullen as Janet, Andrew Cruickshank as Dr. Cameron, and Bill Simpson as Alan

Dr. Finlay's Casebook

The first of a twelve-part series based on a character created by A. J. Cronin

7.55 OF all the doctors who have written about their calling, **A. J. Cronin** has undoubtedly made the greatest impact. *The Stars Look Down, The Citadel, The Keys of the Kingdom*—these and other best-sellers have all become equally successful films. And tonight this world-famous author reaches his largest audience yet as BBC-tv presents the first episode in a new series based on his stories *The Adventures of a Black Bag*.

The year is 1928 and the place Glasgow. Alan Finlay, a hard-up young medical student with a passionate ambition to become a surgeon, is only a few weeks away from his final exams when he becomes involved in the strange disappearance of his landlady's husband. Finlay, with all the confidence of a student, ventures an opinion, and by chance finds himself in conflict with the veteran, Dr. Cameron. It is a chance which is to shape his career.

An intensive search was made to find a new face to interpret Alan Finlay. Playing the part in the twelve fifty-minute programmes of the series will be **Bill Simpson**, a young actor whom Scottish viewers will have seen as a newsreader. His experience also includes productions at the Glasgow Citizens' Theatre, and an appearance in *Z Cars*.

Dr. Cameron, the former surgeon now in general practice, is played by that fine Scottish actor **Andrew Cruickshank**. Other regular characters in the series are Janet, Dr. Cameron's housekeeper (**Barbara Mullen**) and Mary, another student (**Geraldine Newman**).

As each episode in the series is a self-contained story, guest stars will appear from time to time. Tonight they are **Joyce Heron, Helen Christie,** and **Alan MacNaughtan**.

GREAT SCOTS

Set in the late 1920s in fictional Tannochbrae, *Dr Finlay's Casebook* was a warm-spirited drama series that wasn't afraid to tackle social issues. Viewers quickly took its three leads to their hearts: Bill Simpson as young Dr Finlay, Andrew Cruickshank as his crusty partner Dr Cameron and Barbara Mullen as their resourceful housekeeper Janet. The regular cast was rounded out by Eric Woodburn as prickly rival Dr Snoddie (below) and Effie Morrison as gossipy midwife Mistress Niven (bottom)

ANDREW CRUICKSHANK
as Dr. Cameron, senior partner of
DR. FINLAY

7.55

SCOTTISH actor Andrew Cruickshank enjoys playing the rather dry Glasgow doctor in *Dr. Finlay's Casebook*. 'It is always satisfying for an actor like myself to get back to the country of his roots,' he explained. What are those roots? In the Depression he left his father's hotel in Aberdeen to learn his craft, playing Shakespeare first in the provinces and later in London; a highlight was a walk-on part in the memorable Paul Robeson production of *Othello*.

In 1937, while at the Old Vic, he appeared in his first television play—as Banquo to Sir Laurence Olivier's Macbeth—from the Alexandra Palace. The war interrupted his career, but while still a major in the Royal Welch Fusiliers he received a letter from Emlyn Williams inviting him to portray the famous Elizabethan actor, Burbage, in *Spring 1600*, in which Rupert Davies also had a part.

This was followed by a succession of roles in the West End and abroad.

'I have always been lucky,' he told me. 'My parts have been in plays that I have liked, plays with moral intimations, almost a moral atmosphere.'

This is why Cruickshank enjoys appearing in plays by Robert Bolt and Graham Greene, admires Alun Owen, and relished playing the severe father in the BBC-tv production of *The Barretts of Wimpole Street*.

These are all fairly serious parts, but this is not surprising for Cruickshank is deeply committed to his art; his wife, Curigwen Lewis, is an actress; and their eldest daughter (they have three children) is soon going to drama school. When not in the studio (we are seeing him more and more on television these days), Cruickshank will be immersed in other aspects of his profession; he is writing a history of the relationships between actors and dramatists, *Westward from Athens*, and is a council member of Equity, the actors' trade union.

GEORGE TREMLETT

31

Radio Times
The Sixties 1962

CHANGING TIMES

Dr Finlay's Casebook ran for eight series between 1962 and 1971 – making the transition to colour television. Of 191 episodes made, 122 are now missing from the BBC archive; however, hundreds of photos from those lost productions are retained in the *Radio Times* vault – many taken by Don Smith. For years, *Dr Finlay* was made at TV Centre in London, with frequent trips to film on location in Callander in Stirling, which stood in for Tannochbrae. In later years, the entire series was produced in Scotland so *RT* commissioned Glasgow-based photographer Robert L Nicholson to record the cast at work

Bill Simpson: Television's Alan Finlay
The story of the man who plays the young doctor

THERE is quite a lot of Dr. Finlay in **Bill Simpson**, the young Scottish actor who has made his mark in the successful adaptation of the **A. J. Cronin** stories, *Dr. Finlay's Casebook*, which ends tonight (with the possibility of a second series next year being considered); so, he admits, is Bill Simpson. Finlay came to a professional life from a background of farming; so did Simpson. He was born in Ayr, and spent his young years working on his grandfather's farm in the region near Glasgow where 'Tannochbrae' is set.

Simpson left the farm for the R.A.F. and moved thence to a 'pretty dull job' in an insurance office. He had never done any acting even on the amateur stage but on an impulse he applied for a grant at Glasgow's College of Dramatic Art. One important reason for this move was that, like all good Scotsmen, he hankered after further education and, as he says, 'this was one college which didn't ask for an impressive list of school credits I hadn't got.'

The grant obtained, and the course completed, he joined the Gateway, the Edinburgh repertory theatre. During two seasons there, he managed to fit in his first television work from the BBC's Glasgow studios. He followed this with a part in Sir Tyrone Guthrie's notable production of the Scots classic *The Three Estates*.

Work in the Glasgow Citizens Theatre and a spell as a television newsreader came next, and then on another impulse he decided to take a holiday in London. But no Scotsman worth the salt in his porridge has ever come to London just for a holiday—as every Boswell fan knows. In any case, Simpson soon turned up in a *Z Cars* episode and immediately afterwards landed the Dr. Finlay part.

Now he intends to stay in London. 'I loved working in the Scottish theatre but it's really a very small world up there, and I'd like to do everything there is to be done in acting,' he says. So he has settled in Kensington, but hearing all round him the expensive accents for which the district is noted he does not think he will ever learn to play an Englishman.

GREAT RECIPE
Main picture: Andrew Cruickshank, Barbara Mullen and Bill Simpson photographed for a March 1967 *RT* cover
Right: a profile of Barbara Mullen from a 1964 *RT*

Barbara Mullen

SHE is small and sweet and very feminine, with a soft accent so enchanting that you wonder how Dr. Cameron could possibly have failed to fall in love with her the moment she arrived in Tannochbrae. But then, as she says with a characteristic touch of practicality: 'In a doctor's house, one has to keep both feet firmly on the ground. It is the scene of so many dramas, so many comedies and tragedies, that without a solid anchor of commonsense you couldn't run the thing at all.'

Janet, that anchor of Arden House, supposedly came from a Hebridean farm as a young girl to go into service with Dr. Cameron. Barbara Mullen, by way of contrast, came from Boston, Massachusetts, to lead a life so full of living that she could publish her autobiography when she was still eighteen.

Her father had emigrated to America from the rocky Aran isles, off the Irish coast, to be in turn a wool packer, labour organiser, and a notable distiller of home-brewed whisky during the thirsty years of Prohibition. When Pat Mullen returned to the islands (he later became famous as the *Man of Aran* in Robert Flaherty's classic documentary film) Barbara, as befitted a member of a 'roaming, roving family,' set off for London and drama school.

It was in 1938 that she first appeared on BBC television, dancing in an Irish programme from Alexandra Palace. A year later she had caught the critics' attention as a precocious ten-year-old boy in a West End revue. Within another year she was established as the star of *Jeannie*, and a success she has remained—on the stage, in many films, and particularly on television both sides of the Atlantic.

As Janet in *Dr. Finlay's Casebook*, she has made a most emphatic hit. 'I think the core of it is that she is a very real and human character. Do you recall the episode where she walked out on her two doctors? A housekeeper wrote to me and said I should really think twice before giving up such a good position . . .'

A real-life Janet would find it hard to keep pace with Barbara Mullen. Brimful of vitality, she runs a London flat, a house in Dublin; in company with two daughters helps her husband manage a film unit—and still finds leisure to write plays, go fishing with her brother off Aran, and enjoy a good argument. 'Fortunately I need very little sleep.'

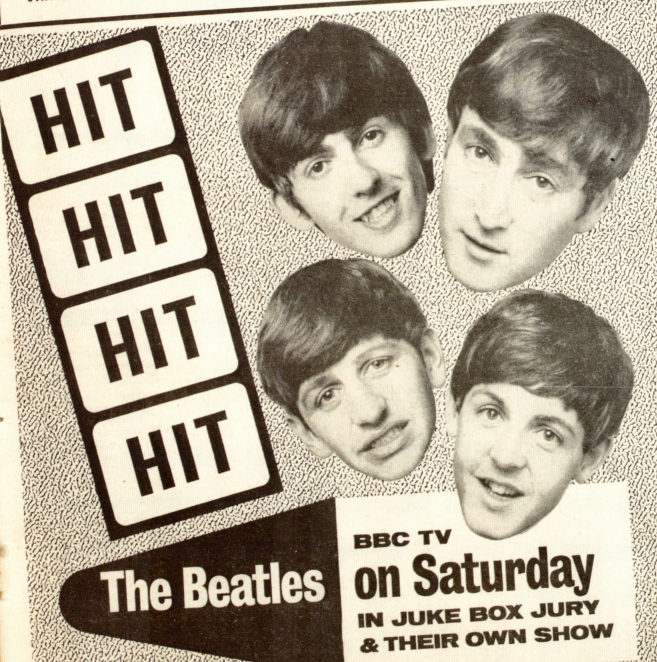

1963

RADIO TIMES December 5, 1963

Your Weekend Saturday

The Beatles ...... TWICE TONIGHT

FAB FOUR
By December 1963, the Beatles were a sensation with two hit albums and two number one singles in the UK charts – and a third soon to follow with *I Want to Hold Your Hand*. There would be many more afterwards. These days the *RT* issue (opposite) is something of a collector's item

6.5 / 8.10 PARENTS with teenagers in the family are advised to sit well back from the TV set: they may get trampled in the rush. And teenagers with parents in the family have a golden opportunity to show them what Beatlemania is all about—even, perhaps, to convert them. For this evening the Beatles have sixty minutes of BBC-tv time to themselves.

First, at five past six, they take over as the jury of *Juke Box Jury*. Rhythm guitarist and spokesman Beatle, **John Lennon**, was a jury member some months ago, when the first thin screams of Beatle fans were beginning to be heard in the land; now he returns with **Paul, George,** and **Ringo** under the chairmanship of **David Jacobs**.

Secondly, at ten past eight: *It's the Beatles*, in which the group will be playing many of their own favourite numbers and some new ones, and showing their individual talents as well. Among the numbers: the current Beatle hit, *I Want to Hold Your Hand*.

Both programmes will be staged at the Empire Theatre in Liverpool—*It's the Beatles* being recorded in the afternoon— before a capacity house of some 2,500 gathered for the Northern Area Convention of the Beatles National Fan Club. Mobile television cameras will roam the theatre, because as producer **Neville Wortman** says: 'The group's contact with their audience is remarkable to see. The programmes will be virtually a study in Beatlemania.'

Note for Beatle fans: *The Beatles will top the bill in a two-hour radio show on Boxing Day in the Light Programme. Also, there are still some copies of the Radio Times Portrait Gallery photograph of The Beatles available—price 2s., post free, from: BBC Publications (B.T.), Box 123, Queen's House, Kingsway, London, W.C.2.*

Radio Times The Sixties 1963

The Beatles

RADIO TIMES September 12, 1963

RADIO TIMES PORTRAIT GALLERY

PAUL McCARTNEY
Bass guitar, joint composer with John.
Born Liverpool, June 18, 1942

JOHN LENNON
Harmonica, rhythm guitar, composer.
Born Liverpool, October 9, 1940

RINGO STARR
Drums (newest member of group).
Born Liverpool, July 7, 1940

GEORGE HARRISON
Lead guitar.
Born Liverpool, February 25, 1943

'Very much a do-it-yourself outfit'—the secret of the Beatle Cut

If you would like a print of the photograph on the facing page please turn to page 28

JUST how they got their name, even they themselves are not quite sure, although it could have something to do with the fact that they emerged on to the pop scene from a Liverpool cellar club called The Cavern. But there is no dark secret about a success story so big that these days it seems show-business is overrun with Beatles.

Although their average age is only in the lowest twenties, these young musicians are solid professionals. The three founder Beatles—John Lennon, Paul McCartney, and George Harrison—cut their musical eye-teeth on washboards back in the skiffle-happy days of 1956 when they were still at school. For six years they played their way in and around Liverpool, riding the skiffle and rock regimes, collecting en route drummer Ringo Starr and a fiercely loyal following on Merseyside and points north.

Just twelve months ago they cut their first disc, *Love Me Do*. There was no detectable rush on the record shops, but then in January the Beatles burst out all over with *Please, Please Me*. It climbed to the top of the charts, stuck there for four weeks, and earned them a Silver Disc. It was joined by another three months later for *From Me to You*. And only recently they were up among the best-sellers again with *Twist and Shout*, the first EP disc ever to reach the Top Ten.

Very much a do-it-yourself outfit, the Beatles play their own compositions (over a hundred to date), write their own lyrics, score their own arrangements. Equipped with brooding good looks, they inspire devotion of traffic-jam proportions among their fans wherever they appear. If imitation be indeed the sincerest form of flattery, the number of eyebrow-level Beatle haircuts to be seen around the coffee bars is flattery indeed.

Their special plaintive sound is easily recognisable, but less easy to define. Some detect a transatlantic influence, others talk of a unique brand of rhythm-and-blues peculiar to Liverpool. Most, though, are content to call it the Merseyside Beat, switch on the record player, and forget all about definitions. As, indeed, do the Beatles themselves.

The last word is with John Lennon: 'People are always trying to pin labels on us . . . but as far as we're concerned it's just good fun.' It sounds that way—and clearly the sound will be around for a long time to come.

Next week: LOUISE DUNN ('Iris' of 'Compact')

RADIO TIMES September 12, 1963

The Beatles

POSTER BOYS

In September 1963, underestimating the force of Beatlemania, the staff at *Radio Times* were inundated by requests when glossy 8 x 10 inch prints of this photo were offered for the princely sum of two shillings

Your Weekend Sunday

The Madhouse on Castle Street

DYLAN GOES DRAMATIC

In the middle of the Big Freeze of 1963 (one of the coldest winters on record), a 21-year-old American folk musician called Bob Dylan was invited to the UK and cast as Bobby the Hobo in *The Madhouse on Castle Street*.

Evan Jones, the writer of this one-hour *Sunday-Night Play*, later revealed that, in rehearsals, Dylan immediately deferred to the actors, saying, "I don't know what I'm doing here. I can't act." His part was reworked with dialogue going to a new character, Lennie, played by David Warner, while Dylan (pictured second right) performed songs as Lennie's friend, Bobby.

Madhouse was recorded by the BBC but shown only once on 13 January 1963 and subsequently junked. Fan audio recordings of Dylan's songs survive in private hands.

Left to right: David Warner, Bob Dylan, Maureen Pryor, James Mellor, Ursula Howells and Reg Lye

9.0

'I HAVE decided to retire from the world. I shall leave your name with Mrs. Griggs, my landlady, who will notify you when I die. Please arrange for my burial, as I do not wish to trouble the occupants of the house more than is necessary.' The ominous letter from the brother whom she has not seen for fourteen years brings Martha Tompkins to his boarding-house in Castle Street — only to find that Walter has locked himself in his room and is slowly starving to death. But why? Has he committed some crime? His fellow boarders, Bernard the truck driver, Lennie the student, and Bobby the guitar-playing hobo, together with Martha and two strange visitors, try to unravel Walter's secret — and in so doing find themselves revealing the secrets of their own past

The Madhouse on Castle Street is the third play for BBC-tv by **Evan Jones**, following *The Widows of Jaffa* and *In a Backward Country*. His film scripts include *The Damned*, which has yet to be released, and *Eve*, which stars the outstanding French actress Jeanne Moreau in her first English-speaking part.

In **Philip Saville's** production, Martha Tompkins is played by **Ursula Howells**, while **Maureen Pryor** is cast as Mrs. Griggs the landlady and **James Mellor** as Bernard.

Appearing as Bobby the hobo is **Bob Dylan**, brought over from America especially to play the part. Only twenty-one, he is already a major new figure in folk-music, with a reputation as one of the most compelling blues singers ever recorded. The song for which he is best known is 'Talkin' New York,' about his first visit to the city in 1961. A skilled guitarist, his special kind of haunting music forms an integral part of tonight's strange play.

POINTS FROM THE POST

Haunting Guitar

I WOULD like to say how much I enjoyed the excellent BBC-tv play *The Madhouse on Castle Street*. I found the whole production compelling from start to finish, and the characters were all extremely well portrayed.

But the best part of the play was the haunting guitar music of Bob Dylan. It was some of the most interesting and original playing we have had the pleasure of hearing on any medium for a long time.—(Miss) *Jennifer M. Dunbar, Harrow.*

37

The Year That Was

Going out live on Saturday nights, *That Was the Week That Was* was a key player in the satire boom of the early 1960s. Lampooning the week's news, the series had launched late in 1962 and, by 1963, become must-see TV – especially once the Profumo scandal was making headlines.

Led by anchorman David Frost, the witty regulars (above) posed for *RT*'s Don Smith during rehearsals for the edition on 12 January 1963. Then, on 19 March, Smith took solo portraits of Millicent Martin (right), the actress and singer who belted out topical numbers in every show.

Contrary to expectations voiced in the article (opposite page), *TWTWTW* came off air in December 1963, with the BBC mindful of the 1964 general election. It would never resume but was influential for decades to come.

RADIO TIMES September 26, 1963

Your Weekend Saturday

David Frost

Millicent Martin

Lance Percival

William Rushton

Roy Kinnear

10.30 WIELDING a voice that has been described as having the sharpest cutting edge in the business, **Millie Martin** will make the first incision at approximately ten-thirty tonight. The only certainty about the proceedings thereafter is that it will be a considerable carve-up, as the rest of the team pounce on the oddities and idiocies of the Week that Was and leave it shredded on the studio floor.

From cabaret, revue, variety tours, summer shows, and film studios they've been rounded up and corralled in Television Centre: **David Frost, Kenneth Cope, David Kernan, Roy Kinnear, Al Mancini, Lance Percival, Bernard Levin**, old uncle **Rushton** and all. Joining them tonight are two newcomers: **Irwin Watson**—spotted by *TWTWTW* producer **Ned Sherrin** at the Apollo Theatre in Harlem, New York—and **Robert Lang**, a young actor from the National Theatre Company.

The first season of *TWTWTW* was planned to run for six weeks, then extended to thirteen, and finally lasted for twenty-three. This time it will run straight through until next April. Just in case there is anyone around who hibernated during the last Big Freeze and does not know what it is all about, we quote what Ned Sherrin describes as 'my splendid sentence which I always trot out: "It's an attempt to turn into television terms the sort of witty conversation you would hope to find in relaxed circumstances late on Saturday night, in the curious sort of no man's land between one week and another where you can afford to sit back and take the mickey out of the past seven days".'

The mickey-taking is, as he insists, a team job in which there are no stars, and the ultimate credit must go to the writers. 'Quite the biggest of our breakthroughs has been that so many people distinguished in other fields—the theatre, novels, and particularly journalism—have written for us so regularly and so well.'

Daring Young Men

FOR my television money the healthiest and most daring programme, which I definitely would not miss on a Saturday night, is *That Was The Week That Was*.

Praise be to the young people who dare the wrath of the dull-witted and pompous to give the public something different, brilliant, and ruthless.

May this lively, sane, yes even ridiculous programme go on for ever. —(Mrs.) F. J. Lewis, Bristol 8.

IN common with many others I had long thought that the BBC was entirely subject to the dogma of the gospel according to St. Richard Dimbleby, and accordingly I was astounded that the BBC should introduce such a programme as *That Was The Week That Was*.

This is a programme that was really needed by this country—long may it continue!—John G. H. Kirkpatrick, Orpington, Kent.

LOOSE CANNON TWTWTW was devised by satirist Ned Sherrin (above). From 1986 to 2006, he hosted Radio 4's entertainment round-up *Loose Ends*

Radio Times
The Sixties 1963

RADIO TIMES *November 21, 1963*

Your Weekend **Saturday**

DR. WHO

In this series of adventures in space and time the title-role will be played by William Hartnell

📺 **5.15** DR. WHO? That is just the point. Nobody knows precisely who he is, this mysterious exile from another world and a distant future whose adventures begin today. But this much is known: he has a ship in which he can travel through space and time—although, owing to a defect in its instruments he can never be sure where and when his 'landings' may take place. And he has a grand-daughter Susan, a strange amalgam of teenage normality and uncanny intelligence.

Playing the Doctor is the well-known film actor, **William Hartnell**, who has not appeared before on BBC-tv.

Each adventure in the series will cover several weekly episodes, and the first is by the Australian author **Anthony Coburn**. It begins by telling how the Doctor finds himself visiting the Britain of today: Susan (played by **Carole Ann Ford**) has become a pupil at an ordinary British school, where her incredible breadth of knowledge has whetted the curiosity of two of her teachers. These are the history teacher Barbara Wright (**Jacqueline Hill**), and the science master Ian Chesterton (**William Russell**), and their curiosity leads them to become inextricably involved in the Doctor's strange travels.

Because of the imperfections in the ship's navigation aids, the four travellers are liable in subsequent stories to find themselves absolutely anywhere in time—past, present, or future. They may visit a distant galaxy where civilisation has been devastated by the blast of a neutron bomb or they may find themselves journeying to far Cathay in the caravan of Marco Polo. The whole cosmos in fact is their oyster.

WHO IS THE DOCTOR?
The very first episode found the enigmatic Doctor (William Hartnell) and his police box Tardis in a London junkyard

Birth of a legend

In 1963, *RT* photographer **Don Smith** took some of the very first publicity shots of *Doctor Who*. As the studio sets for the first episode, *An Unearthly Child*, weren't ready, the photoshoot used mock-ups of a classroom and a junkyard, suggesting the settings that would be seen in the episode. "Oh yes, I remember it well," Smith told *RT* in 2013. "I took them in the photographic studio in the basement at Television Centre, which was just a large room – most uninspiring. We had bits of furniture in the waiting room, and it was just a matter of dragging anything in."

William Hartnell had a reputation for being testy, but Smith said, "In the period he was Doctor Who, I had quite a lot to do with him. I always found him OK. He was never tetchy with me. I'd always say to him, 'William, please may I take a picture of you doing this or that?' and I don't ever remember him saying no."

Smith also recalled that, a few weeks later in 1963, "one of the BBC publicity photographers, Douglas Playle, a dear friend, said to me, 'I've just been down to Lime Grove photographing an episode of *Doctor Who*. And they've got these fantastic things – they're like inverted dustbins on wheels. It's fantastic the way they move about.' Doug said, 'I can see them becoming very popular and being the in-thing.' I've often thought back on that."

The Daleks were coming…

Dr. Who
📺 SATURDAY's serial begins when two teachers (**Jacqueline Hill** and **William Russell**) probe the mystery surrounding one of their pupils (**Carol Ann Ford**)—and meet the strange Dr. Who

RADIO TIMES *November 21, 1963*

SATURDAY BBC tv
NOVEMBER 23

5.15
DR. WHO
An adventure in space and time
with
WILLIAM HARTNELL
as Dr. Who
WILLIAM RUSSELL
as Ian Chesterton
JACQUELINE HILL
as Barbara Wright
and
CAROLE ANN FORD
as Susan Foreman
An Unearthly Child
by ANTHONY COBURN
Title music by RON GRAINER and the
BBC Radiophonic Workshop
Incidental music by NORMAN KAY
Story editor, David Whitaker
Designer, Peter Brachacki
Associate producer, Mervyn Pinfield
Producer, VERITY LAMBERT
† Directed by WARIS HUSSEIN
See page 7

5.40
THE TELEGOONS
Peter Sellers
Harry Secombe
Spike Milligan
BBC radio's
world-famous Goons
in a new puppet series
for television
This week's adventure is:
The Canal
Script by SPIKE MILLIGAN
Television adaptation by
Maurice Wiltshire
Produced by
TONY YOUNG of Grosvenor Films
for BBC-tv

5.55
THE NEWS
and
THE WEATHER MAN

6.5
JUKE BOX JURY
A new disc—a Hit or a Miss?
Comment and opinions on
the latest pop releases
This week's panel:
Cilla Black
Sid James
Don Moss
Anna Quayle
In the chair, David Jacobs
Programme devised by Peter Potter
Presented by Neville Wortman

6.35
DIXON OF DOCK GREEN
starring
JACK WARNER
A series created by TED WILLIS
The Switch
Written by ARTHUR SWINSON
P.C. George Dixon........JACK WARNER
Mary Crawford
            JEANNETTE HUTCHINSON
Det.-Sgt. Andy Crawford
                       PETER BYRNE
Sgt. Flint................ARTHUR RIGBY
Mr. Enderby............CHARLES LAMB
Cadet Michael Bonnet...PAUL ELLIOTT
Inspector Bob Cherry
                    ROBERT CAWDRON
Mr. Holdsworth......RICHARD COLEMAN
Dino Pia..................JOHN BENNETT
Pam............ELIZABETH CHAMBERS
Skerritt................DONALD MORLEY
Margaret.............BETTY ENGLAND
Det.-Constable Lauderdale
                   GEOFFREY ADAMS
Mrs. Venables........MARY HIGNETT
W.P.C. Alex Johns........JAN MILLER
P.C. Jones................JOHN HUGHES
Bill........................PAUL TAYLOR
Don.........................JAMES BECK
Carol..................SANDRA CARON
W.P. Sgt. Chris Freeman
                        ANNE RIDLER
Mrs. Rose................DOROTHY DARKE
Film cameraman, Arthur Smith
Film editor, Valerie Best
Designer, Austen Spriggs
Directed by DAVID ASKEY
† Production by RONALD MARSH

7.20
WELLS FARGO
New adventures of
DALE ROBERTSON
as Special Agent Jim Hardie
in
Death Raffle
with
Jack Ging, William Demarest
Former confederates of reformed outlaw Dave Heweitt use his affection
for a crippled girl to force him to
assist with a bank robbery.

David Frost
AND
Bernard Levin
in another edition of
That Was The Week That Was
AT 10.20

8.10
THE SATURDAY FILM
presenting
Santa Fe Passage
A Western
starring
JOHN PAYNE
FAITH DOMERGUE
and
ROD CAMERON
Directed by William Witney
Kirby Randolph............JOHN PAYNE
Aurelie St. Clair......FAITH DOMERGUE
Jess Griswold............ROD CAMERON
Sam Beckman............SLIM PICKENS
Ptewaquin..................IRENE TEDROW
Satank....................GEORGE KEYMAS
Pioneers moving west along the Santa
Fe trail are facing a full-scale Indian
uprising. But in spite of the desperate
odds of the desperate, Kirby Ran-
dolph, is determined to settle his own
score with the treacherous Indian Chief
who is responsible for the attacks.

9.35
COMEDY PLAYHOUSE
by HARRY DRIVER
and JACK ROSENTHAL
The Chars
starring
ELSIE and DORIS WATERS
with
ANN LANCASTER
Cissy....................DORIS WATERS
Flo........................ELSIE WATERS
Amanda................ANN LANCASTER
Cyril, bus driver.....MICHAEL BALFOUR
Sydney, conductor.........JAMES BECK
Frank, commissionaire
                  ARTHUR LOVEGROVE
Other chars.............BETTY AUBREY
      GRACE NEWCOMBE, BETTY CARDNO
Mr. Thornton............DEREK NIMMO
Incidental music composed and
conducted by RON GRAINER
Designer, John Cooper
† Production by DOUGLAS MOODIE
See page 7

10.5
NEWS
SPORT

10.20
THAT WAS THE WEEK THAT WAS
It's over, let it go—but not
before it's been mutilated with
relish by
DAVID FROST
and
MILLICENT MARTIN
KENNETH COPE
DAVID KERNAN
ROY KINNEAR
BERNARD LEVIN
AL MANCINI
LANCE PERCIVAL
WILLIAM RUSHTON
Musical numbers staged
David Harding
Musical director, DAV
Designer, Stuart Dura
Producer, NED SHERRI
It is regretted that no ti
can be considered for thi

11.10
THE WEATHER
Close Down

Monte Cristo cream, shipped by BURGOYNE'S from sunny Cyprus
9/- A BOTTLE

Monte Cristo cream
BURGOYNE'S
& CO. LTD. LONDON E.1

CHEAP-TRUNK-CALL DAY TOMORROW!

Ring them up tomorrow.
It's Sunday—and cheap
calls all day long.
ON S.T.D—
worth-while calls for 1/-
or even 6d!
VIA THE OPERATOR—
save up to 1/9 on a
3 minute trunk call!

SHOCK NEWS
There were big names in the BBC's line-up for Saturday 23 November 1963 but broadcasts were overshadowed by the assassination of US president John F Kennedy the day before. *Doctor Who's* debut went ahead but was repeated the following Saturday for those who had missed it. *That Was the Week That Was* ditched all its satire and produced a shorter, 30-minute tribute to JFK

NOVEMBER 21—27

Radio Times (Incorporating World-Radio) November 19, 1964. Vol. 165: No. 2141.

BBC-1
tv
BBC-2

Radio Times
LONDON AND SOUTH-EAST
SIXPENCE

DR. WHO AND THE DALEKS
SATURDAY TV

1964

RADIO TIMES *November 19, 1964*

THE DALEKS ARE HERE!

1 **5.40** WHIRLING through space and time *Tardis* touches down at the start of today's new *Dr. Who* adventure on dry land where, according to Susan's reading of the instruments, it is 'radiation nil, oxygen normal, pressure normal —an earth reading!'

And it is, in fact, London. A menacingly hushed London, with no sign of life and an eerie feeling of decay. Once again the time factor is in doubt, for Dr. Who and his companions could have landed in the early 1900s— or the twenty-fifth century. But having discovered where they are, they soon realise *when* they are, for the city is not as empty as it appears to be. Some startling visitors from another planet have also landed on earth, and the travellers find themselves facing antagonists whom they had thought destroyed. . .

When the Daleks were first introduced on television last spring in a story scripted by **Terry Nation**, they were an instant hit with young viewers, and not a few parents too. Over a thousand letters arrived at the BBC asking whether the squat robots with the tinny voices could be borrowed or bought. Such was the demand that, on *Blue Peter*, instructions were given for making a do-it-yourself Dalek, and two of the original specimens were given to the children of Dr. Barnardo's Homes.

Currently, the robots are multiplying like rabbits in readiness for Christmas, when Dalek books, badges, sweets, and both small battery-powered and full-size child-powered versions are due in the shops. As far as we can discover these are *not* packed complete with easily assembled Realistic Death Rays ('Super Holiday Fun: Disintegrate Your Dad!'), so parents may rest easy. Although, on the other hand, you-can-ne-ver-tell-what-a-Da-lek-might-get-up-to. . .
PHILIP BLAKE

Dr. Who Knows

SINCE the first episode I have watched BBC-tv's *Dr. Who* on Saturdays, with great intensity. I think the series is extremely good and very realistic.

When an idea occurs in my mind that a certain fact is impossible the schoolteacher Mr. Chesterton usually voices it and it is immediately expelled from the mind by Dr. Who, who asks: 'Why is it not possible?' and gives a credible explanation.

The sensible way in which they think out the problems is much better than all the uncontrollable dashing around, getting further and further involved, which so often happens in science fiction.

I hope we can have more excellent programmes like this.—*(Miss) Janet F. Harris, Leeds, 17.*

Boo to Dr. Who!

MAY I respectfully suggest that Janet F. Harris (RADIO TIMES, February 6) needs her head examining?

Several members of our form (the sixth) have to watch *Dr. Who* with younger brothers and sisters, and all agree that after *Steptoe* it is the funniest programme on television.

The 'Daleks,' which looked like salt and pepper pots with knobs on, and had voices like a bad telephone, were hilarious. 'Then—this-is-the-end-of-the—Daleks,' at which their rubber suckers sagged, left me in fits of laughter (my friends experienced similar reactions).

There is nothing realistic about this serial. Even the acting is 'hammy,' and it does not deserve the name of science fiction.—*Lillian Roberts, Chorley, Lancs.*

EXTERMINATE!

The Daleks had made a such huge impact in their *Doctor Who* debut the previous winter that a rematch was guaranteed. This time they had escaped their home world Skaro and were determined to subjugate planet Earth

Below: a selection of letters from the *Radio Times* mailbag as *Doctor Who* gained some of its earliest fans and critics

Dr. Who for All?

MAY I respectfully suggest that Lillian Roberts (RADIO TIMES, February 27) needs *her* head examining.

My husband, myself, and four children aged 17, 15, 12, and 4½ all thoroughly enjoy *Dr. Who*, and think it has, up to now, been a very clever programme. — *Jean Glazebrook, Rosudgeon, Cornwall.*

Radio Times
The Sixties 1964

NEXT WEEK *in Radio Times*

Dr. Who AND THE DALEKS

In the new adventure beginning on Saturday the Doctor comes face to face again with those familiar mechanical monsters— the Daleks

DALEK MANIA
Left: the Daleks were captured in cartoon form by *RT*'s stalwart artist Cecil W Bacon
Below: in the Christmas 1964 *RT*, readers could see the Daleks and the Doctor (William Hartnell) in colour for the first time. The young woman meeting them was Babs Lord, later a dancer in Pan's People

'He's got slight indigestion,' said Dr. Who, 'you'll probably get it yourself. Now open your mouth'

A BIG WEEK FOR BLUE PETER

1 **5.5** GOOD news for *Blue Peter* fans—no need to wait a whole week for the next programme. On Thursday a regular second edition begins with the same team as the Monday programme—**Christopher Trace**, **Valerie Singleton**, and of course **Petra** and **Jason**. The only missing member of the team will be **Fred** the tortoise, cosily packed away for his winter hibernation.

Chris and Valerie have already had some amazing adventures on *Blue Peter* and you can be sure there are many more surprises in store, for instance, they are both entered as co-drivers of a 1901 Durkopp in this year's London-Brighton run.

With two programmes a week there will be more opportunity to include some of the very good ideas sent in by winners of *Blue Peter* badges. Badges are also awarded for interesting letters, models, drawings, and paintings, and to competition winners. On Thursday there is a chance to enter a special competition and win one of the new *Blue Peter Annuals*, so make sure you have a paper and pencil handy.

The behind-the-scenes team will split up for the new plan. **Edward Barnes**, recently back from the Far East gathering material for a future series, will direct the Monday programme. **Rosemary Gill**, who filmed the story of Valerie's flight to Lagos in the VC10, will direct on Thursdays.

We often have letters from young viewers asking, 'Can I join the Blue Peter Club?' The answer is that if you watch *Blue Peter* you are already a member. **BIDDY BAXTER**

TWICE AS GOOD
In September 1964, *Blue Peter* editor Biddy Baxter alerted young viewers via *RT* (left) that the show was going twice weekly. Hosts Christopher Trace and Valerie Singleton are pictured with guide dog Honey Below: Valerie Singleton, photographed for *RT* shortly after joining *Blue Peter* in 1962

'I like it when things go wrong'

Graduating from Rada in 1956, **Valerie Singleton** fast became a face of the 1960s and a household name on the BBC. But, she tells *RT* in 2022, it's largely forgotten that she made commercials on ITV. "They were like advertising magazines, little 15-minute soaps with a story built around them, and every now and then they'd say, 'Oh, I've just bought this wonderful new shaver,' and hold it to camera."

She soon moved to "the other side". "I was invited to the BBC Club for a drink by the people in charge of presentation and taken on as an in-vision continuity announcer in the afternoons. There were a few of us – Judith Chalmers, who's still around, and Val Pitts, who went on to marry the conductor Georg Solti." Singleton had to write her own links between programmes, "but because everything was live, you'd suddenly find your 30-second piece cut to 20. Or you might have to expand it. I was so good at timing for a while."

One day in 1962 she bumped into an old chum, Christopher Trace. "He said, 'Listen, I do this programme called *Blue Peter* – 15 minutes once a week all about trains.' I'd never heard of it. 'Would you like to audition?'" She bagged the co-presenting job a few months later but was still working as an announcer. "So I ran the risk of saying, 'And now over to me in the *Blue Peter* studio.'" Singleton had to choose. "*Blue Peter* seemed more fun because it was often out and about. But it was a very small programme then."

Under the aegis of a new producer/editor Biddy Baxter and directors Edward Barnes and Rosemary Gill, *Blue Peter* quickly expanded in its remit and ambition, going twice weekly in 1964.

"I loved it when *Blue Peter* went live," says Singleton, ever unflappable when mishaps occurred. "I rather like it when things go wrong. One week Christopher was allowed to go on holiday so it was just me doing the show. I had a piece on Guy Fawkes, and the floor manager was mouthing at me, 'We haven't got any film.' So I was ad-libbing my way through the whole programme. At the end there was a tremendous sense of satisfaction. And Biddy clippity-cloppity-ed down the stairs and said, 'Well done!' I just find live television more challenging and exciting."

For Singleton, one of the key pleasures of the show was "entertaining children, encouraging them, letting them know what else was going on in the world". But it didn't come easily. "The first time I went to a school fête, I was terrified. The teacher said, 'Can you talk to the children?' And I thought, 'What am I going to talk about?' Then they said, 'Could you make something?' I thought, 'I don't make things. [Craft expert] Margaret Parnell makes things. Not me.' Another thing that always drove me mad was people saying, 'Do you like children?' It's ridiculous. People never say, 'Do you like grown-ups?' Some kids I liked and enjoyed spending time with. Other kids I couldn't abide. I liked my friends' children. Never had my own."

She remains justly proud of *Blue Peter*'s many achievements during her ten-year tenure – from training guide dogs for the blind to the annual charitable appeals. "We always spaced it out so there'd be one at home and one abroad. It taught children about all sorts of things like the Biafran war and helped them be involved."

She moved on from *Blue Peter* in 1972 but even now, 50 years later, is constantly recognised. "I'm always being stopped. People say, 'I loved your programme. Thank you so much.'" She finds it gratifying. "It's the people I meet who say, 'I'm a dress designer because of *Blue Peter*' or 'I make glass because of *Blue Peter*' or 'I'm a painter because of *Blue Peter*'. It seems, unknowingly, we were encouraging people into all sorts of ways of life. That's really nice."

TITTER YE NOT!

Comedy legend Frankie Howerd larked about on the *RT* cover several times. In December 1964, he was launching a new BBC1 show with long-time collaborators Ray Galton and Alan Simpson

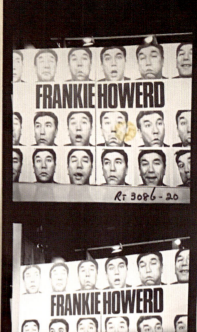

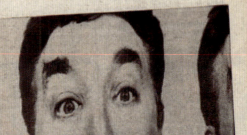

Friday

1 8.0

'Ten a.m. Rang Frankie Howerd at home. Had just left for rehearsal. Rang rehearsal hall. F.H. in middle of scene. Would I call back? Rang producer **Duncan Wood**. Busy in conference. Went to library to look up file on F.H., with crisp assessment in mind.

'Hour later, still boggling at bulging file. Mr. Francis Howerd clearly defies pigeon-holing. In recent years has been seen coquettishly flouncing through *Charley's Aunt*, holding the floor in a solo hour at the Establishment Club, spinning gags in radio Variety, playing at the Old Vic (to quote Ned Sherrin: " the best and funniest Bottom one will ever see "), sending up the Budget on *TW3*, performing the same service recently for the General Election. For past fifteen months has been starring in West End in *A Funny Thing Happened on the Way to the Forum* as, of all things, a Roman slave.

'Abandon crisp assessment, ring rehearsal hall. Line engaged. Try Duncan Wood, make contact, request summing-up of series. Reply: " By and large, it's just the *Frankie Howerd* show." Make intelligent noise, venture to ask for amplification. " You could call it situation comedy," says Wood patiently, " but Frank is not playing a character, simply himself. Throughout the show he maintains contact with the viewing audience." About to suggest further chat over luxurious meal at producer's expense, when Wood called away on urgent business.

'Ring rehearsal hall. F.H. gone for lunch. Make do with solitary canteen sandwich. Decide to seek illuminating quote from writers, responsible for seven *Hancock* series, two *Comedy Playhouse* series, three *Steptoe* series. Dial number, ask to speak to Alan Simpson or Ray Galton. *Two* voices answer: " Speaking." Suppress image of double-headed comedy writer, and somehow get involved in discussion on non-working.

'Says Ray Galton (or Alan Simpson): " We have more methods of non-working than any other writers in the business. We get to the office at about ten-thirty, and by a carefully mapped out programme of non-work we needn't start until three or four in the afternoon. Talking to you like this is an ideal form of non-work . . ."

'Grope for assessment of F.H. Says Alan Simpson (or Ray Galton): " The great secret of anything Frank does is his gossipy approach and his ability to reduce, say C. P. Snow's *Corridors of Power* to the importance of a Noddy book." And the series? " Well, we're just trying to be funny, really. You won't find any deep message in *our* scripts."

'Decide to find script and extract some small message for readers. Take Tube to TV Centre, and on arrival ring rehearsal hall. Line engaged. Track down script of first programme, reach for cup of tea; phone rings and harassed Radio Times voice says: " Deadline in fifteen minutes. For goodness' sake what's the *Frankie Howerd* Show about?"

'Fumble with script and hopefully read at random from page where television executive is telling Frankie Howerd: " It's up to you to stop the rot. Restore responsible broadcasting to this country, take up the sword of the BBC, lead them back to their rightful pre-eminence in this green and pleasant land."

'Radio Times voice says: " Oh." Only possible comment, really.'

You may imagine that a 'Radio Times' man sent to investigate a new series has only to have a luxurious lunch with the producer, a cosy chat with the star, a word or two with the writers, and voilà!— a fact-packed piece of prose which tells you just what you'll see when you switch on. Sometimes it doesn't quite work out that way; as witness Philip Blake's running report on a day spent investigating

THE FRANKIE HOWERD SHOW

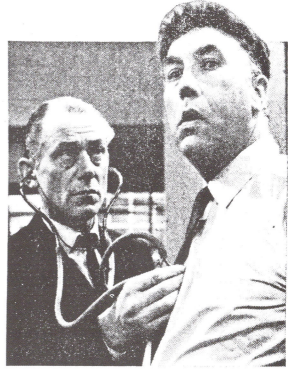

'Dr.' Patrick Cargill examines Frankie

Frankie with the scriptwriters—Alan Simpson (left) and Ray Galton

Radio Times
The Sixties 1964

Take 2

The build-up to a second BBC television service had been protracted and widely publicised, despite BBC2 initially being available only in the Greater London area and across parts of south-east England. It wouldn't be until the end of the decade that BBC2 could extend its reach to 80 per cent of the UK.

In the event, launch night on Monday 20 April 1964 was a disaster, thanks to a power failure in west London that blacked out Television Centre. Scheduled programmes (including a spectacular production of *Kiss Me, Kate*, starring Patricia Morison and Howard Keel, and *Off with a Bang*, a fireworks display from Southend) could not be shown. Instead, the transmission eventually cut to an emergency broadcast from the BBC Television News headquarters at Alexandra Palace.

Thus, BBC2 had something of a soft launch the following day at 11.00am with the very first edition of *Play School* (opposite page). Of course, the advent of BBC2 meant that the already existing BBC TV channel had to be rebranded BBC1.

OFF WITH A BANG

A grand fireworks display to celebrate the opening of BBC-2 will be shared by viewers on BBC-1

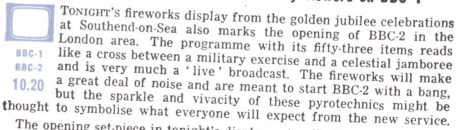

BBC-1
BBC-2
10.20

TONIGHT'S fireworks display from the golden jubilee celebrations at Southend-on-Sea also marks the opening of BBC-2 in the London area. The programme with its fifty-three items reads like a cross between a military exercise and a celestial jamboree and is very much a 'live' broadcast. The fireworks will make a great deal of noise and are meant to start BBC-2 with a bang, but the sparkle and vivacity of these pyrotechnics might be thought to symbolise what everyone will expect from the new service.

The opening set-piece in tonight's display naturally features kangaroos, but there are also a host of other animals whose relevance to Southend or television will be less apparent. The programme enumerates some of them: 'screaming screech owls flying through the air; fiery aigrettes and birds of paradise; a flight of lace-wing moths drifting towards the sea; the screeching parakeets; a large elephant, walking with life-like movements, squirting fire from his trunk, and swishing his fiery tail.' And there are many more besides.

There are also to be salvos of forty shells, barrages of twenty mines, batteries of one hundred and eighty Roman Candles, fire-wheels, elaborate set-pieces, and pyramids of revolving fountains—Bang! Bang! Bang! until the final 'Grand Girandole' which is produced by the simultaneous discharge of a barrage of mines, salvos of shells, and aerial maroons releasing golden orions, humming stars, silver aigrettes, and echoing reports.

Five cameras, two of them on the pier, will capture this display for viewers. In charge of the operation is **Alan Chivers** of BBC-tv, one of whose commitments was last year's Snowdon climb. On that occasion rain nearly ruined everything. Tonight he and his BBC colleagues will be keeping their fingers crossed for fine weather and a fine display—not to speak of the officials and citizens of Southend who are celebrating its fiftieth year as a borough.

RADIO TIMES April 16, 1964

Tuesday

Duke Ellington
with his Orchestra opens a new series
JAZZ 625

2 **9.40**

THERE is nothing so difficult as a beginning, as Byron once pointed out, but the new BBC-2 jazz programme gets off to a really flying start this evening with the music of Duke Ellington and his Orchestra. Ellington's band recently completed one of the most successful tours in living memory. Critics and public were once agreed that Ellington's music was the finest that could be found anywhere in the world of jazz, and it was a happy coincidence that the orchestra's presence in this country should have coincided with early plans for the new BBC television jazz programme.

Ellington, born 1898, still going strong, has been a successful bandleader for forty years, and although he is a highly gifted jazz-pianist it is Ellington the composer who will be remembered by posterity. He has written suites based on Shakespeare's characters and on John Steinbeck's, on the history of Liberia, and on different kinds of perfumes.

Introducing Ellington and his musicians, and resident compère for the series, is **Steve Race**, fresh from his triumphs on radio's *The Jazz Scene*. During the weeks that follow Steve and producer **Terry Henebery** will be presenting the work of several local groups, besides sharing with viewers the pleasure of meeting some of the American virtuosi who have followed Ellington over to Europe.

In the next few weeks Oscar Peterson, Dave Brubeck and the Modern Jazz Quartet will be among the attractions in the series. As for tonight—the Duke Ellington Orchestra. No jazz series in history could ever have had a more distinguished curtain-raiser.
— BENNY GREEN

LEGEND
After the power failure on BBC2's launch night, Duke Ellington on *Jazz 625* was undoubtedly the highlight of the second night. British jazz saxophonist Benny Green introduced it for *RT*

GOAL!
BBC2 also originated *Match of the Day*, first as a Wimbledon tennis package, then turning to football on 24 August 1964. Two years later, the show switched to BBC1

AT 6.30 ON BBC-2 Match of the Day

Match of the Day

2 **6.30**

TODAY for the first time soccer fans can watch a feature-length version—as opposed to a potted 'highlights' version—of a regular League fixture. Which one? That, by agreement with the Football League, remains a secret until 4.0 this afternoon. But Bryan Cowgill, BBC-tv's sports chief, promises that it will be a top match

The agreement by which BBC-tv won permission for this came after careful negotiations between Bryan Cowgill and League Secretary Alan Hardaker. It allows for fifty-five minutes of coverage, enough to show the whole development of the game, and for its screening at a more popular hour.

'Up to now we have only been able to show ten-minute edited films of any given match, which effectively meant a machine-gun succession of goal-goal-goal,' says Cowgill. 'Now we can fall in line with BBC-2's policy by offering "depth" treatment of our most popular sport.' To those who think this breakthrough is a further blow to turnstile takings, he offers his experienced opinion that 'television never kept anyone away from the best in sport.'

In charge of the new venture as producer is **Alan Chivers**, BBC-tv's most experienced soccer specialist. He intends to make full use of the technical advantages of 625 lines, and says: 'We're no longer restricted mainly to the close-up. With 625's greater definition we can use wider shots without losing clarity, and so show much more of the overall pattern of a game.'

2 **11.0 a.m.**

Joy Whitby introduces her new BBC-2 series beginning today which provides a 'nursery school' for the under-fives

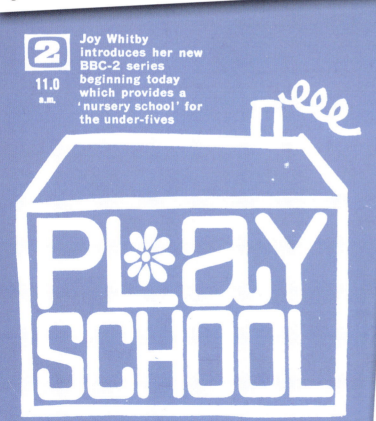

RADIO TIMES PORTRAIT GALLERY

Dusty Springfield

WOMAN OF SOUL
On New Year's Day 1964, Dusty Springfield kicked off the first-ever *Top of the Pops* with *I Only Want to Be with You*. Often dubbed "Britain's greatest soul singer", by 1966 she was hosting her own BBC1 show, *Dusty*

Radio Times Portrait Gallery

Week by week Radio Times is featuring portraits of the stars (opposite). As a service to our readers glossy 10 in. by 8 in. photographs are available, PRICE 2/- *post free. If you would like one please fill in this coupon, cut out and send it with a crossed postal order for 2/- to:*

BBC PUBLICATIONS (D.S.)
P.O. BOX 123, LONDON, W.1.
N.B. This is your self-addressed label so please write clearly in ink

The Dusty Springfield photograph

NAME _____

ADDRESS _____

_____

_____

BLOCK LETTERS PLEASE
We regret that we cannot supply photographs other than those in Portrait Gallery

---

WHEN Mary O'Brien was ten her teacher asked her what she would like to be: she said she wanted to be a blues singer. 'I didn't know what that was,' she says now, ' but I thought it sounded good.' Ask any jazz musician and he might tell you that the blues are the cry of a sad soul's experience of life—a sombre ambition for a ten-year-old! Yet Dusty Springfield, the twenty-four-year-old woman into whom that school-girl grew has almost realised this ambition—as close as the pop idiom will allow.

And perhaps her life has brought to the voice a unique and contemporary quality that brings the blues within the reach of today's teenagers. Dusty's voice was once accurately defined—' as if it were on its way to a prayer-meeting and got lost in Tin Pan Alley.' Music has always been a consuming passion for her and in particular American Negro music; even an untutored ear can detect the influence of coloured singers on her style—a debt that Dusty is only too ready to acknowledge.

But there is something else there too; the chastening experience of show business on a young girl who had to sacrifice a private life to an ambition. ' I never had any normal teenage life because I was interested only in singing,' she will tell you. ' I've never been to a night club except to work and I've never been in love.' Yet the fruits of success are sweet and Dusty would not give them up for the cosy bliss of a semi-detached—for all her hankering after normality.

Blisteringly honest, Dusty Springfield confesses to being short-sighted, having ' khaki-coloured eyes,' to being a worrier and a thrower of crockery. In her time she has been a char, sold dustbins, and served behind a counter. She has a horror of growing old; she emulates the kooky looks of model girls; and she is given to such dubious public statements as ' Sometimes I think it's easier to do well as a singer if you're working class.'

But most important, Dusty has, in the eleven months since the Springfields went their separate ways, established herself as one of the most exciting and most consistent girl singers on the pop scene today, even if—for the sake of her career—she studies to be ' the kind of girl another girl would leave her boy friend with.'

NEXT WEEK:
The Rolling Stones

The Rolling Stones

Radio Times — The Sixties 1964

> **PARENTS BEWARE**
> At the same time as making them poster boys, in 1964 *RT* was examining the Stones' "primitive" appeal. Pictured from left: Brian Jones, Charlie Watts, Bill Wyman, Keith Richards and Mick Jagger

'Would You Let Your Daughter Marry A Rolling Stone?' This headline in a trade paper speaks volumes: its humour camouflages the outrage of a generation of parents who have weathered Johnny Ray's tears, Elvis Presley's gyrations, and The Beatles' dandified falsettos only to see their youngest screaming for a quintet of ravers next to whom the rest look like choir-boys. The Stones even inspire ambivalent reactions in their own following: one columnist received a letter which read—'I want to put weed-killer in Charlie Watts's tea. P.S. I love The Stones. No offence meant.' Drummer Charlie was too busy with his collection of pocket handkerchiefs to take offence.

Love 'em or hate 'em, you just can't be indifferent towards The Stones. With The Beatles now firmly gathered to the bosom of the Establishment The Rolling Stones have taken over as the symbol of youth in revolt. Anti-parent, anti-social, and anti-barber, they are—as their manager would have us believe—not so much a group as a 'way of life.' For the boys they're scruffy, primitive, and 'it's impossible to push them around.' For the girls they're as cuddlesome as Shetland ponies and infinitely more menacing.

With grammar school or art school educations, hailing variously from Dartford, Cheltenham, and London, the Stones play down their Home County background—especially Mick Jagger who gave up his studies at the London School of Economics to embrace the New Brutality. Yet this thuggish image is peddled to the press with little reference to the facts. The revelation of Bill Wyman's marriage and his baby son came like a cold douche of cologne on the group's reputation. Another set-back occurred at a hotel pool in Texas during their American tour when myopic locals mistakenly ogled them as girls in one-piece bathing suits!

The group took their name from the song 'Rolling Stone Blues,' sung by the great shouter, Muddy Waters, and their style derives directly from the harsh, raw blues of early jazz via Bo Diddley and Chuck Berry. On stage The Stones generate a primitive excitement that has incited their fans to riot (at Lord Bath's country estate). By their own estimation their life in the pop world will be short. Now that they've been voted Britain's top vocal and instrumental group they have little to be brutal about. The big question is—after The Rolling Stones who comes next?

...and that pretty stewardess you've been chatting-up

GLASSES FULL
Globetrotting Alan Whicker had been filing *Whicker's World* reports on the BBC's *Tonight* programme since the 1950s. It led to his own series and he became a regular *RT* contributor

RADIO TIMES July 23, 1964

WHICKER'S WORLD

'Tonight' is on holiday—but there's no rest for globe-trotting Alan Whicker. This article is the first of three in which he harvests memories and impressions of his journeys in the past seven years. Later, other seasoned BBC travellers will write about their experiences

The world's a small place when you're roving around in the big jets; six miles up, travel is a mixture of boredom and indigestion. Flying to Australia, almost keeping up with the sun, the time difference means that as fresh passengers come aboard at New York, San Francisco, Honolulu and Fiji, the clock goes back —and they keep *on* serving you dinner. A man can take just so many of those predigested trayfuls, punctuated by white boiled sweets.

Apart from those damn sweets, everything *else* has changed, up there. When I started my travels without the benefit of uniform, just after the war, the flight to Tokyo in an Argonaut (210 m.p.h., pushing it) took three days, with a nightstop in Calcutta. By the time you arrived, passengers and crew were old friends in a sort of intrepid, jolly flying club.

Today you hurtle through space at 600 m.p.h., speechless amid a hundred strangers. You're travelling so fast there's rarely more than three or four hours between airports; then you get new passengers, new crew, and that pretty stewardess you've been chatting-up is replaced by an aloof girl who's in love with the navigator.

Impersonal and boring as an international Green Line it may be, but at least (I keep telling myself) it's *safe*. In smaller aircraft on obscure local airlines, one can feel less secure. In Mexico, bumping along seven thousand feet above Aguascalientes, someone recalled that our aircraft had been bought in a job-lot several years before, after being rejected as too old and unserviceable by an *Oriental* airline . . . All of a sudden, I went very quiet.

52

Radio Times
The Sixties 1964

THE OLYMPIC GAMES
FROM TOKYO via Satellite

TOKYO 1964
The 18th Olympiad got under way in October – a huge operation for BBC TV and Radio. Victor Reinganum, who'd first contributed to *RT* in 1926, painted an evocative cover including Japan's rising sun and symbolic birds of goodwill

THE OPENING CEREMONY
Tonight at 10.25

The ninety-seven nations competing parade around the National Stadium **The Emperor of Japan** declares the Games open The Olympic flag is raised; the pigeons, carrying messages of goodwill, are released; the Olympic torch arrives and the flame is lit One Japanese athlete, representing all the competitors, pronounces the Olympic oath and the Olympic Games are under way

SERIOUS LAUGHS
Iconoclast playwright Joe Orton had shaken up West End theatre in May 1964 with *Entertaining Mr Sloane*. In August 1964, he introduced his latest radio play to *RT* readers – and addressed the matter of taste

The Ruffian on the Stair

THIRD 8.0

If you weigh my play *The Ruffian on the Stair* in the balance of good taste you will find you have been short-measured. It concerns a young thug called Wilson who nurses an incestuous passion for his brother, recently murdered. Wishing to commit suicide but deterred by religious scruples, he calls at the home of Mike, the man he suspects of being his brother's murderer. He terrorises Joyce, Mike's mistress, and achieves a devious revenge.

Ten years ago this theme would have provided an addition to that moribund theatrical genre, Strong Drama. Since the mid-fifties playwrights have forsaken the inshore fisheries for the ocean proper. Today it is farce.

In a world run by fools the writer can only chronicle the doings of fools or their victims. And because the world is a cruel and heartless place, he will be accused of cruelty and heartlessness. If he thinks that the world is not only cruel and heartless but funny as well, he has given his critics an extra brickbat to fling and will be accused of not taking his subject seriously.

But laughter is a serious business and comedy a weapon more dangerous than tragedy. Which is why tyrants treat it with caution. The actual material of tragedy is equally viable in comedy—unless you happen to be writing in English, when the question of taste occurs. The English are the most tasteless nation on earth, which is why they set such store by it.

JOE ORTON

53

MARCH 10 TV WEDNESDAY

MARCH 6—12

BBC-1

Radio Times
SIXPENCE

LONDON AND SOUTH-EAST

tv

BBC-2

Radio Times (Incorporating World-Radio) March 4, 1965. Vol. 166; No. 2156.

NOT ONLY... BUT ALSO

SATURDAY, BBC-2

Production team, Hugh Duggan
Bob Murray, Philip Mutton
Producer, RONALD WEBSTER
From the West

* Approximate time
† BBC recording

1965

NOT A DUD… BUT A HIT

BBC2 was at the cutting edge of comedy in 1965 with *Not Only… but Also*, a vehicle for *Beyond the Fringe* alumni Peter Cook and Dudley Moore. Such was their cachet that John Lennon appeared in a 1964 pilot and the first edition televised on 9 January 1965. *RT*'s Don Smith caught them on set, together with actor Norman Rossington (right), in some now slightly water-damaged photographs

Radio Times
The Sixties 1965

CHRISTMAS
DUD AND PETE
By Dudley Moore and Peter Cook—featuring themselves in character

PETE: All right, Dud?

DUD: All right, Pete, nothing like a nice cup of tea, especially when it's laced with a splash of V.P. 5-star—it warms the cockles of the heart, warms you right through.

P: Yes, in the Festive Season what could be more appropriate?

D: Wonderful, isn't it, Pete, in the Festive Season, when Robin Redbreast sings his roundelay of cheer.

P: Robin Redbreast symbolises the Xmas spirit to me.

D: And he does for me, Pete.

P: The trouble is that you don't see any robins in England at Christmas time.

D: You see them on Christmas cards though, don't you?

P: Yes, they're all drawn by Australian artists, because that's where the robins go for Christmas. Australian Christmas must be wonderful, with all those people surfing in with the Christmas pudding on trays.

D: Marvellous that, ain't it?

P: But do you think we're going to have a white Christmas this year?

D: I hope so, Pete, because I'm looking forward to making the traditional snowman, and throwing a few snowballs at Greenlane Primary School windows.

P: Lovely crisp snow, it's part and parcel of a wonderful Christmas, isn't it?

D: It certainly is, Pete—holly looking lovely and green.

P: Yes, I can never find any holly with berries on it. 'Course, it's largely due to the robins, 'cos it's a long flight to Australia, and they usually take a few berries with them . . .

D: . . . to keep them alive on the way . . .

P: Strapped to their legs. As you know, the spider weaves his gossamer threads through night and day and the robin, when he sees a berry in mid-flight, well, he feels like a berry and so he sees a berry on a holly and he can't carry it in his beak all the way, so he gets the spiders to tie the berries to his legs with their webby substances.

D: It's wonderful the way those spiders help out, you know, when robins are in need of a bit of help, there they are weaving away . . .

P: If only human beings, Dud, could behave towards each other the way spiders do to robins.

D: If only that could happen, Pete, then peace would reign on earth.

P: And U Thant would be out of a job again.

D: Exactly, Pete. Well, anyway, Christmas as you know comes but once a year.

P: And when it comes it brings Aunt Dolly.

D: Yeh, that is the only thing I dread about Christmas, that it brings Aunt Dolly.

P: Well, you have these seasons and you have to extend your charitable facilities.

D: Yes, but after a few glasses of light ale she starts extending her charitable facilities along Lymington Crescent at the top of her voice.

P: Well, of course, you know it is the season of goodwill to all men and she takes a somewhat literal attitude towards this old saying.

D: Last year I thought she was a bit of a disgrace. I mean, she came out of the Royal Oak reeking of stout and I didn't get a look in at the chicken.

P: Well, she is a voracious woman, Dud, there's no doubt about that . . .

D: What are you going to do this year, Pete? Are you going to put some decorations up?

P: Well, you know I don't like buying things. You know I like to make my own decorations. 'Cos if you use your imagination you can get wonderful things like, er . . . well, if you take some potatoes and dip them in silver paint and you stick some . . . stick some . . .

D: A couple of berries in for eyes . . .

P: Yes, a couple of berries in for eyes and you take a carrot for the nose and you cover that with frosting . . .

D: It's wonderful, Pete. I do a very similar thing with cornflakes. What I do is I dip them in some tinsel which I have smeared with seasonal honey and when I bring the Christmas pudding in and set light to it with paraffin, I throw the cereals over it.

P: What a lovely thought.

D: It is a lovely thought, Pete, but it ruins the taste of the pudding, that's the only thing.

P: Yes, well, you know you can't have everything.

D: You can't, Pete, you can't. I think you've either got to have the colour or the tastiness, not both.

P: The thing I like is the Christmas crackers you get, some of those jokes they have in the crackers. Whoever does those, he's a wonderful wit.

D: And it's the work of one mind, Pete, it isn't a group of people, it's the work of one mind because they've all got that same stamp of hilarity.

P: I'm told it's the Duke of Edinburgh does it.

D: I wouldn't be at all surprised, Pete.

P: What are you going to give for presents this year?

D: Well, I've given you a pen and pencil set. . . . Whoops, I've let it out.

P: Where? You haven't let it out, it's in the cupboard upstairs. I've seen it.

D: Oh, you've seen it. I put it behind the apricot jam. I didn't think you'd see it there.

P: Well, I was looking for a place to hide my gift to you.

D: Is it hankies again?

P: It's not the same hankies, no. No, I bought you some underpants with the wines of the world all over them, you know, they have pictures of bottles of beaujolais on and bottles of champagne and it gives you a sort of festive feeling under your trousers.

D: Are you sending any cards this year, Pete?

P: No, I'm taking out an advertisement in the Dagenham Advertiser, saying that I am not sending cards this year, but instead am making a small contribution to the 'Clean-Up TV' fund.

D: A very wonderful idea, Pete. Well, I think I'd better be getting back.

P: If you look out of the window you can see the first flakes of snow.

D: It's going to be a white Christmas, Pete.

P: Or perhaps it's Mrs. Woolly shaking her head out of the window again.

D: Well, whatever it is, it's settling, Pete.

**Radio Times
The Sixties 1965**

CRACKERS

PETE & DUD
Peter Cook and Dudley Moore often performed as the flat-capped duo from Dagenham – and wrote a dialogue as those characters (opposite page) for the 1965 Christmas *Radio Times*

Radio Times The Sixties 1965

RADIO TIMES May 6, 1965 31

Tuesday

'I, CASSIUS'
presents a new, intimate portrait of the extraordinary man

BEHIND THE MOUTH

 9.25

'YOU'RE awfully lucky to do a programme like this with me. I don't know any other heavyweight champion who would have done it.' These were among the last words spoken by Cassius Clay to **Harry Carpenter** and myself when we left Miami Beach after a week's filming. Clay was right. We were lucky to find this unpredictable man so co-operative, and we were equally fortunate to be able to build a programme around such a fascinating character.

Never before has a programme of this nature been presented. *I, Cassius* probes into the nature and background of the reigning world heavyweight champion.

No one has ever made such an impact on the sporting world as Cassius Marcellus Clay. Perhaps his boastful eloquence more than his deeds, his extravagant claims to be 'the greatest' and 'the prettiest,' first made him world famous. He provided so many glib headlines that they tended to overshadow the fact that here was a man who did precisely what he set out to do. No ordinary man becomes world champion at twenty-two years of age after only twenty professional fights.

Clay has never been predictable since he won a Gold Medal at the Olympic Games in Rome in 1960. He was sponsored as a professional by a group of millionaires, and he went on to shatter accepted sporting patterns. After he had won the world heavyweight title, he shook America by embracing the Muslim faith —and thereby throwing away a fortune. He insists now on being called by his new name, Muhammad Ali.

It was impossible to work to any set plan because the champion is a law unto himself. One morning he would start his roadwork when it was still pitch-dark and we would be following him around unable to shoot a foot of film. The next morning he would wait for the dawn and we would be able to film. As the days passed he became more co-operative and talked frankly about his younger days.

We went to Louisville in Kentucky where he was born. We talked to his mother and to people who had known him as a boy. They all helped to fill in the picture of a man who is much more than just the 'big mouth' his publicity made him out to be. LESLIE KETTLEY

Cassius Clay with his wife

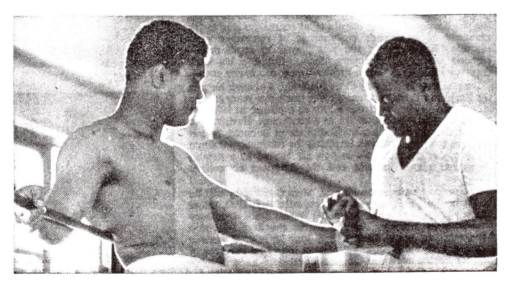

The champion with friends and in training for his return fight with Sonny Liston on May 25

KNOCKOUT

In 1965, even BBC sports producer Leslie Kettley and commentator Harry Carpenter (writing for *RT*) were adjusting to the fact that Cassius Clay had recently converted to Islam and renamed himself Muhammad Ali. As for the long-awaited rematch with Sonny Liston... Clay/Ali knocked him out in the first round

THE HEAVYWEIGHT CHAMPIONSHIP OF THE WORLD

Cassius Clay v. Sonny Liston

The long-awaited contest can be heard as it happens in America in the Light Programme early this morning—and seen in a film on BBC-1 this evening

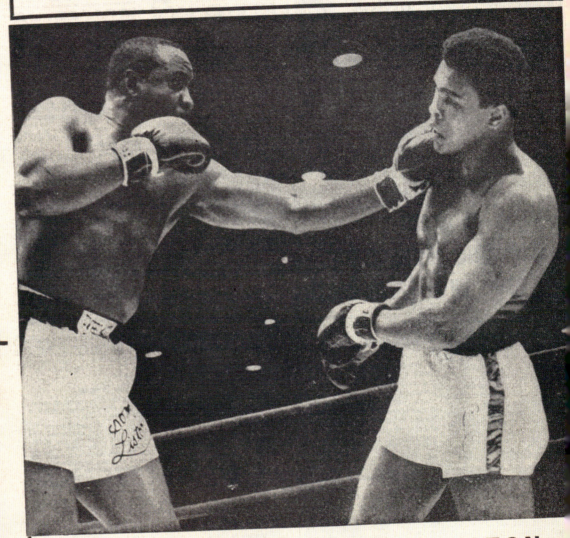

Radio Times (Incorporating World-Radio) May 20, 1965. Vol. 167; No. 2167

Radio Times

SIXPENCE   LONDON AND SOUTH-EAST

MAY 22—28

BBC-1   tv   BBC-2

CASSIUS CLAY v. SONNY LISTON
The World Heavyweight Championship in the Light Programme and on BBC-1 (See page 39)

LIGHT 3.25 a.m.
BBC-1 9.0

THIS is where we came in . . . all set for Cassius Clay, alias Muhammad Ali of the Muslim faith, to defend his world heavyweight crown against Charles Sonny Liston, the once-feared ex-champion now widely and prematurely regarded as a tiger turned tabby-cat.

Just where we were six months ago in Boston on a rainy Friday night, seventy-two hours before the fight, when Hal Conrad, the bony, bespectacled, and long-suffering journalist who (heaven help him) publicises the Clay-Liston promotions, yelled the news at press H.Q.: 'Clay's ill, fellas, the fight's off!'

So here we go again, with the protagonists six months older but possibly not wiser. The half-year lapse is important because at Liston's time of life, which is anything from his official thirty-one to perhaps seven or eight years older, every passing month is another nail in the coffin of his useful fighting life. He was very fit last time. Can he endure the training grind again?

I was with Clay at his Miami house recently, making the documentary *I, Cassius* which was shown on BBC-1 on May 11, and apart from the inevitable fat which rolled up during his convalescence, he looked good. In the week I was there, the fat began to melt under the heat of hard work.

For those of us who could hardly believe what we saw the first time they fought, fifteen months ago, prophecy is difficult this time. Can Liston, even at his age, be as bad as he looked then, when he permitted the contemptuous Clay to paw him in the face? Who could foresee that Liston would stay stuck to his stool after six rounds and plead a damaged shoulder?

Of course, it may be simple. Maybe Clay is a clever young boxer, exceptionally fast for his fifteen-and-a-half stone, and has the beating of Liston every time. Or perhaps Liston this time will show some of the savagery which destroyed poor Floyd Patterson twice within a round.

HARRY CARPENTER

LADDISH HUMOUR

RT photographer Don Smith vividly recalled *The Likely Lads*. "That's my favourite show of all time. It really is. From the moment it started, I thought, 'Wow!' Because I would've been in my early 30s, and the lads were supposed to be early 20s, I'd just gone through that stage. And I could identify with it. I became quite friendly with James Bolam and Rodney Bewes [who played Terry and Bob], and with the writers, Dick Clement and Ian La Frenais. I made a point of trying to photograph every episode."

THE LIKELY LADS

The BBC-2 comedy success starring James Bolam and Rodney Bewes comes to BBC-1

1 8.0

THE LADS—Bob Ferris and Terry Collier—are around twenty-one. They have twelve or maybe fourteen pounds a week. They like the town because it is the place they know best. They are acquainted with every back street, pub, and club, and such useful arts as getting into the Palais without a pass out. They are acquisitive and irreverent, but with their own strain of idealism and a good strong shot of Northern common sense.

James Bolam (Terry) and **Rodney Bewes** (Bob) are both from the North. While they are not necessarily like the Lads they know their type very well. Bolam comes from Sunderland and was articled to a chartered accountant before he set out for London and the Central School of Drama. He 'arrived' with North-country neo-realism in the English cinema, and he had important parts in *A Kind of Loving* and *The Loneliness of the Long Distance Runner*.

Bewes is from Bingley in Yorkshire. Acting proved to be a cure for persistent asthma: bedridden and always away from school he dreamed of becoming an actor. An audition for a children's television serial provided him with the opportunity he needed. He went to R.A.D.A. where, to use his own phrase, he was 'chucked out.' He is now twenty-six, and made a name for himself when he appeared as Tom Courtenay's mate in the film *Billy Liar*. In television he has appeared in *Z Cars, Dixon,* and *Cluff*.

In tonight's episode Terry, in spite of Bob's misgivings, tries to pick up not one, but two girls.

Radio Times The Sixties 1965

RADIO TIMES September 30, 1965

Tuesday

THE NEWCOMERS

A twice-weekly serial about Londoners moving with their factory to the country

Maggie Fitzgibbon as Vivienne, Jeremy Bulloch as Philip, Alan Browning as Ellis, and Gladys Henson as Gran

 7.0 ELLIS COOPER, shop superintendent of a firm making components for computers, tells his wife Vivienne that his factory is moving to a sleepy country town in East Anglia and he has been offered promotion to works manager. Vivienne, city born and bred, a modern woman, marriage counsellor, content with her home and social circle, quails; her elder son, Philip, faced with changing sixth forms, hates the prospect; Maria, aged sixteen, keen on riding, romantic about the country, sides with her father; Lance, thirteen, the problem of the family, a cinema fan frequently asked to remove himself from the auditorium, imagines himself roaming the woods shooting game.

Angleton—don't look for it on the map, but it exists—has been invaded many times since the Romans. Half the younger generation have left town by the time they are twenty-one; a penny on the rates fails to raise a hundred pounds; unemployment is above the national average. The council, realising their town would die in a few years, have invited new blood.

They know rich agricultural land will vanish for ever under bricks and mortar, and the days when everyone knew everyone in the High Street will end. There will be strangers, used to buses every five minutes, expressing eloquent dissatisfaction with the lack of amenities.

For the 'strangers' on new housing estates there is loneliness, fear, and boredom. There are also new boy friends, new girl friends, new babies, feuds with farmers, brittle industrial relations, and civic intrigue—copious material for the twice-weekly serial, *The Newcomers*, on Tuesdays and Fridays.

COLIN MORRIS

UNITED!

A twice-weekly serial set in the exciting world of League Football

1 7.0 ASSOCIATION FOOTBALL, the made-in-Britain sport which has grown into the world's foremost ball game, can provide almost every element of drama. Matches are themselves action dramas; the struggle of the game as a whole to survive in its country of birth in the face of diminishing 'gates' is another kind of drama. Comedies and tragedies are played out in the rivalries between players, the conflicts of players with managements, the opposing claims of club and family loyalties.

The new twice-weekly (Monday and Wednesday) serial opening today aims to exploit these possibilities by following the fortunes of one fictional club, 'United' belongs somewhere in the Midlands, and has just taken on a keen young manager whose task is to try to lift the club from its precarious position at the bottom of the Second Division. Gerry Barford, played by **David Lodge** (right), is responsible to the club's chairman, Ted Dawson (**Robin Wentworth**), and has to cope with his ingratiating secretary, Frank Silby (**Arnold Peters**). He also has domestic responsibilities: to his wife Mary (**Ursula O'Leary**) and to his son Kevin, an ambitious young footballer.

Then there are the players themselves, among them Jack Birkett, Jimmy Stokes, Mick Dougall, Kenny Craig, and Curly Parker—each one a distinct and sometimes troublesome personality, and a separate problem for Gerry.

Soap double

Following the demise of twice-weekly soap *Compact* in July 1965, the BBC drama department was gearing up for not one but two replacements serials: *United!* shown every Monday and Wednesday and *The Newcomers* on Tuesdays and Fridays.

United! starred David Lodge as a football manager and was the less successful of the two, ceasing after 18 months.

The Newcomers was initially produced by Verity Lambert, her next project after her success with *Doctor Who*. It starred Maggie Fitzgibbon and Alan Browning and gave Jenny Agutter and Wendy Richard significant early roles. Hugely popular, it lasted for four years, ending in November 1969, the week before BBC1 went into colour.

PLAYS

CURTAIN UP

As well as long-running series, the BBC drama department remained committed to one-off plays – fresh spins on classics while nurturing such taboo-busting trailblazers as Ken Loach

The single play on television, lamented as dead not so long ago, should prove itself alive and kicking in no fewer than four major series beginning or continuing on BBC Television.

The Wednesday Play, which kept the flag of new committed drama flying last season, starts another season next week, surprisingly—but surprise too is one of its aims—with a 'period' play: *Alice* by Dennis Potter is the story behind the story which Lewis Carroll wrote to bring him lasting fame.

Two other plays by Potter are planned: together they trace the career through Oxford and constituency politics of a naive character called Nigel Barton. A new play, *The Coming-Out Party*, is also promised by James O'Connor, the former convict who wrote *Tap on the Shoulder* and *Three Clear Sundays*—sensations of the last season.

Another TV writing talent, David Turner, will contribute *Way Off Beat*, a look at the ballroom-dancing world. One Wednesday Play will be a musical—*The End of Arthur's Marriage* by Christopher Logue and Stanley Myers.

A more widely spaced series of large-scale productions, with a large cast and important theme, will be **Play of the Month.** The first will be a TV production of John Osborne's *Luther*, starring Alec McCowen. Then come E. M. Forster's *A Passage to India*, starring Sybil Thorndike, and *The Joel Brandt Story*, evoking the background of the Eichmann trial.

On BBC-2 **Theatre 625** continues weekly with classics like *Miss Julie*, new plays like *The Siege of Manchester*, a history chronicle, by Keith Dewhurst, and dramatisations including three from George Orwell—*Keep the Aspidistra Flying*, *1984*, *Coming Up for Air*—climaxed by a showing of the film of *Animal Farm*.

Thirty-Minute Theatre reintroduces the short play—performed live—in a long run which opens this week with *Parson's Pleasure*, based on the story by Roald Dahl.

The series will also include the first TV performance of a Tennessee Williams play, and specially commissioned works by N. F. Simpson, Hugh Leonard, James Hanley, and James Saunders. Writers new to TV will also be introduced.

Up the Junction
by NELL DUNN

1 9.40

'It is not a play, a documentary, or a musical. It is all of these at once'

'THE real thing.' 'Highly accomplished . . . truthful and likeable.' 'Remorseless observation.' 'A new and exciting young writer with an ear for the authentic idiom of the Smoke.' 'Razor quick, abrasive, hugely comic . . .' Those are some critics raving. They were going mad about a little book of a hundred pages by an unknown girl called Nell Dunn—*Up the Junction*.

Three girls go up the Junction—Clapham Junction. This is their story and they happen to live and work in Battersea, although it could be lots of places. A place of dead-end jobs, crumbling houses, dirty streets and, for the sensitive observer, an overwhelming sense of you-never-had-it-so-bad. Whether you like it or not, this is here, now, 1965.

Go to any big city and the human waste will horrify you, because the people you will see tonight are exploited, given a raw deal, or just conveniently forgotten by the rest of us. You would expect them to be 'down'—and they have every right to be. But they are not. All of them—all ages—are irrepressibly alive. And the young people, like Rube, Sylvie, Eileen, and their friends in tonight's play, have a personal style and sophistication which put to shame the self-promoting 'in-groups' with their trendy clothes and their colour supplements.

How to bring this to the screen? So many conventional plays seem unreal, and real people in documentaries often look and talk like actors. I said the other week that we on *The Wednesday Play* would have to break some rules to tell the truth as we see it. So we told our director, **Kenneth Loach**, that none of the sacred cows of television drama need stand in his way. There were many risks involved in this freedom and he has embraced them with relish.

This is a show which defies the categories. It is not a play, a documentary, or a musical. It is all of these at once. It is something new—but, more important, it is something true. If you watch it we can promise you something that will stay in your mind for a long time.

TONY GARNETT

A Passage to India

PLAY OF THE MONTH tonight is a dramatisation of E. M. Forster's great novel. Dame Sybil Thorndike plays Mrs. Moore, and Virginia McKenna plays Adela Quested, the English girl whose relationship with an Indian doctor causes a crisis between the British and Indian communities

Cyril Cusack plays Fielding—a member of the British community who has 'gone native'

1 9.0

THE British once occupied India; they never conquered her. As the oyster protects itself from the grain of sand by sealing it off in a pearl, India briefly tolerated the foreign body in her midst by isolating it culturally and socially. And attempts by either Indians or British to disturb this state of affairs usually bore tragic consequences.

This is the underlying theme of *A Passage to India*, the great novel of E. M. Forster whose dramatised version by **Santha Rama Rau** is tonight's Play of the Month. It tells the story of Miss Adela Quested, an emotionally unstable young Englishwoman brought to India by her prospective mother-in-law, who encounters an Indian doctor named Aziz. He believes idealistically that the two sides can be brought to understanding, and invites the friendship of the two English ladies for this reason. But the inner conflicts of Miss Quested, added to the deep distrust existing between the British and Indian communities, bring about catastrophe and an actual widening of the racial gulf.

E. M. Forster, who is now eighty-six, first conceived this novel in 1911, when he visited India with his Cambridge friend, the critic G. Lowes Dickinson. At that time he had already established a high reputation with two novels written in and about Italy, *Where Angels Fear To Tread* and *A Room With A View*, and with the better-known *Howard's End*. Always a careful and deliberate writer, Forster delayed completing *A Passage To India* until after he had paid a second visit to the country in 1921. The book finally came out three years later.

The dramatic adaptation which Forster sanctioned for the theatre some years ago, and which is substantially the version used tonight, is by a writer especially qualified to understand both the Eastern and Western viewpoints. Santha Rama Rau is herself an Indian, but she is married to an American and divides her time between India and New York. Equally appropriate to the subject is the play's director, **Waris Hussein**. He comes from a Moslem Indian family living in Lucknow, and he took advantage of a recent visit home to film exterior scenes which are used in the play.

The production is an ambitious one, and has an appropriately distinguished cast. Mrs. Moore, the perceptive and sympathetic lady who has brought Adela Quested to India and who is instrumental in exposing her to 'native' society, is played by **Dame Sybil Thorndike**. Miss Quested herself is played by **Virginia McKenna**, star of many important British films, and her fiancé Ronny Heaslop, an all-too-typical 'sahib' whose bigotry has much to do with her emotional tensions, by **Ronald Hines**.

The Pakistani actor **Zia Mohyeddin**, who plays the idealistic Dr. Aziz, repeats the part which he created in the original London stage production. The principal cast is completed by **Allan Cuthbertson**, who plays Mr. McBryde, and **Cyril Cusack** as Mr. Fielding. Fielding is the British head of the government college in the fictional town of Chandrapore where much of the action takes place, and his liberal attitudes have antagonised his European colleagues.

MICHAEL WILLIAMS

Meeting EM Forster

Waris Hussein directed six BBC *Plays of the Month* (1965–75) and nine *Wednesday Plays* (1966–68). He has a particular fondness for his 1965 version of *A Passage to India*, as he tells *RT* in 2022. "I actually went to see EM Forster in Cambridge and he was full of prejudices about film-making. He said, 'I don't want my books touched. I don't want any filming done.' I remember following this little man down the King's Parade as he was elbowing people out of the way."

The author eventually consented to an adaptation of an existing stage version, which Hussein and writer John Maynard reworked for television. To lift the studio-bound production, Hussein filmed several establishing shots while on a trip to India, and he cast Dame Sybil Thorndike and Virginia McKenna in the star roles.

Hussein laments the BBC's policy at the time of junking many of these ground-breaking productions, and he long believed *A Passage to India* lost for ever. "Only by chance, a copy came to light when they were cleaning out Ealing Film Studios. They offered it to me in exchange for my fee for a talk I was to give. I said, 'The money is nothing to me – I want my *Passage to India*!' So we rescued a 16mm film print. Thank God, it had been preserved. I held onto the print myself in my basement and now the British Film Institute has it."

1966

RADIO TIMES July 7, 1966

THE WORLD CUP

The Opening Ceremony

BBC-1
6.50
LIGHT
7.15

FOOTBALL HISTORY

Whether you were alive then or not, 1966 is the World Cup cemented in everyone's consciousness. *Radio Times* set the stage with a memorable cover and (above) an illustration by Victor Reinganum

EVERY sport has its day, its crowded hour when people whose normal interest in it is marginal or even beyond the fringe share its magic with the most dedicated fans. Tonight marks just such a moment in the annals of soccer. If anyone does not know already, Britain is host country for the 1966 final competition for the Jules Rimet World Championship Cup, and Wembley Stadium—the cathedral of English football—is the scene of the opening game. In the presence of Her Majesty the Queen and His Royal Highness the Duke of Edinburgh, England meet Uruguay in the first of the thirty-two matches up and down the country which will decide the Cup holders for the next four years.

For football addicts all over the globe the occasion is charged with almost mystical drama. And even the most casual viewer could be engulfed in the emotional tides generated by the 100,000 spectators on the spot, not to mention the tens of millions participating through TV, radio, and film.

David Coleman will set the scene as ten TV cameras open up on the packed stadium. Fifteen minutes from zero hour comes the flag-bearing ceremony, when 320 London schoolboys march out from the players' tunnel, deployed in sixteen groups of twenty. Each group will wear the team colours of one of the competing countries. Brazil, as holders, will lead the procession round the track to a point in front of the Royal Box. A fanfare from eight State Trumpeters will now mark the entry of the Queen and the Duke of Edinburgh. As they take up position on a special dais the National Anthem will be played by the Massed Bands of the Brigade of Guards.

At the invitation of Sir Stanley Rous, President of the Fédération Internationale de Football Association, the Queen will then declare the competition open. This will be the signal for the England and Uruguay teams to emerge from their tunnel and parade before the Royal dais during the playing of the Uruguayan National Anthem. What follows will belong to football history.

Radio Times · The Sixties 1966

INTRODUCING THE TEAMS

Their chances... their personalities... their problems—seven pages of expert comment and analysis compiled by Kenneth Wolstenholme and Brian Moore

ENGLAND
Group 1
Chances of success have never been brighter

Bobby Charlton

SITTING comfortably in his armchair at home in Ipswich some three and a half years ago, Alf Ramsey told a huge television audience: 'Yes, England will win the World Cup.' He had just been appointed England's team manager and for this rather cautious man it was a surprisingly bold pronouncement. Now that armchair in Suffolk has become the hottest seat in English football. Because now Mr. Ramsey must justify those words.

Certainly England's chances of success have never been brighter. They are host nation and host nations usually do well. Sweden reached the final in front of their own people in 1958, for example; the moderate Chilean side got to the semi-finals four years ago. England will play at Wembley—their 'home' ground where their record has rarely been smudged.

But these are only minor bonus marks to Mr. Ramsey. He knows that in the end it will be the players he chooses, their mood, their form, and the way he asks them to play that will count.

England have been drawn with France, Uruguay, and Mexico. England's last match with France was in February 1963, in Paris, which was lost 5-2 (Ramsey's first match as manager); they beat Uruguay 2-1 at Wembley in 1964, and Mexico 8-0 there three years earlier. The signs are promising.

England are likely, for the most part, to play a 4-3-3 system. So far as it is possible to explain it simply this means that four defenders are strung out to supply immediate cover to the goal, three more work in midfield and are expected to attack and defend, and three more are left forward to strike hard for the opposite goal. This system has begun to bear fruit for England—chiefly in that magnificent 2-0 win over Spain in Madrid in December and again in that highly-promising win with the same score over Yugoslavia at Wembley in May.

Finally who are the men you must watch? Well, you won't help but notice the flowing and fluent movement of Bobby Charlton, Footballer of the Year, the tenacity of his Manchester United team-mate Nobby Stiles, or the gritty defence of his long, lean brother, Jack Charlton. Around them almost certainly will be Bobby Moore and those two fine full-backs, George Cohen and Ray Wilson. And behind them the dependable Gordon Banks in goal.

If there is a serious question mark against England it is that in recent matches they have made too little use of their chances in front of goal.

WEST GERMANY
Group 2
The team that could well be in the final

Karl-Heinz Schnellinger

CHANCES
BBC commentators Kenneth Wolstenholme and Brian Moore assessed all the teams for *RT*. The final, of course, saw England beat West Germany 4–2

'THE OLD FOX,' as they used to call Uncle Sepp Herberger, the West German team manager, no longer holds the reins of control. He has been succeeded on his retirement by Helmut Schoen, who for so long was his assistant. But don't underestimate Schoen. He has been close to Herberger long enough to learn the strategy of 'ignore the results in the intermediate years: just concentrate on winning the World Cup.'

On that strategy West Germany haven't done so badly since they re-entered the football world. In their very first World Cup they pulled off a tactical sensation by playing a reserve team in one match and going on to win the trophy by beating Hungary in the final. In 1958 they finished fourth. In 1962 they were eliminated in the quarter-finals.

That is a splendid enough record, and if you are jotting down likely winners of this 1966 tournament, don't forget West Germany.

At times their trouble is going to be to decide which players to leave out, not which players to include. It is frightening to think that they can choose a forward line from a galaxy of talent including Seeler, the explosive centre-forward from Hamburg; Brunnemeier, the captain of Munich 1860, whose team we saw beaten by West Ham in the European Cup Winners' Cup Final a year ago; Haller and Brulls, who have been playing in Italy; Konietzka, a deadly striker from Munich 1860; Beckenbauer, an excellent midfield player from Bayern Munich; and that sensational Borussia Dortmund trio of Siegfried Held and the flying strikers, Reinhard Libuda and Lothar Emmerich. Behind those star-studded forwards, Schoen can present such defenders as Horst Szymaniak, Willi Schulz, and Karl-Heinz Schnellinger.

West Germany have been showing a gradual improvement ever since the 1962 World Cup. Their team is a mixture of experience and youth, and although it will play the 4-3-3 system it can call upon many fast and dangerous strikers. No country, for instance, can produce wingmen of the calibre of Libuda and Emmerich.

The sight of the competition should be the German attack against the solid Argentinian defence, but, strangely enough, the Germans do not fear either Argentina or Spain more than the Swiss, who are generally regarded as the weakest nation in Group 2. The Swiss have a habit of upsetting the German style of play. But if West Germany beat Switzerland they could head Group 2, and the way would then be open for a West Germany *v.* Brazil final.

At the end of each World Cup competition the commentators and writers begin to nominate their World XI chosen from the players who have taken part in the contest. By the end of July, one man should be every writer's choice. He is Karl-Heinz Schnellinger, the blond twenty-five-year-old German who is equally adept at full-back or half-back.

Schnellinger has already had one big honour. He was chosen to play for the Rest of the World against England at Wembley in 1963.

THESE ARE THE GROUNDS

Wembley
Can hold over 100,000 spectators, but World Cup capacity is limited to 97,000. A new pavilion has been built. Group 1 games—including all of England's—and a quarter-final, a semi-final, the third place play-off, and the final played here.

White City
Capacity for World Cup is 45,000 although the stadium can hold up to 60,000. Just one match in Group 1—France v. Uruguay—played here.

Birmingham
Villa Park, home of Aston Villa. Capacity reduced from over 60,000 to 52,000, but this is because nearly 10,000 seats have been added for World Cup. Pitch widened by three feet. Group 2 games played here.

Sheffield
Hillsborough, home of defeated 1966 F.A. Cup finalists, Sheffield Wednesday. More money — over £200,000 — has been spent on preparing this ground than on any other. Capacity for World Cup about 50,000. Group 2 games and a quarter-final played here.

Liverpool
Goodison Park, home of 1966 F.A. Cup winners, Everton. Ground built in 1892. Over £100,000 spent on improvements for World Cup. With extra seating the capacity is reduced to 62,000. Group 3 games, a quarter-final, and a semi-final played here.

Manchester
Old Trafford, home of Manchester United. Bombed during the war and rebuilt. Capacity will be about 62,000 for the Cup—much the same as usual. Group 3 games played here.

Sunderland
Roker Park, Sunderland's home ground. Capacity of ground reduced from 58,000 to 43,000 by the provision of some 10,000 temporary seats. Group 4 games and a quarter-final played here.

Middlesbrough
Ayresome Park, Middlesbrough's home ground. World Cup improvements to the ground cost over £100,000. Originally capacity was just above the 50,000 minimum required for selection as a World Cup ground. With special seats capacity is well below 50,000. Group 4 games played here.

ENGLAND CHAMPIONS
Martin Peters, Geoff Hurst, captain Bobby Moore, Ray Wilson, George Cohen and Bobby Charlton celebrating at Wembley Stadium on 30 July 1966

Cup Facts and Figures

For the Record

Only one non-Latin nation—West Germany in 1954—has ever won the World Cup. Uruguay (1930 and 1950), Italy (1934 and 1938), and Brazil (1958 and 1962) have all won the trophy twice and need one more victory to make it their own property.

★ ★ ★

If Brazil do win the World Cup—or Jules Rimet Cup to give it its proper name—they will donate another trophy as the World Cup for competition in 1970. And they will call it 'The Winston Churchill Cup.'

★ ★ ★

The individual Cup goal-scoring record is held by Juste Fontaine, of France. He scored thirteen goals in the 1958 competition, scoring in every one of the six games he played. He scored three against Paraguay, two against Yugoslavia, and one against Scotland in the first round; twice in the quarter-final, once in the semi-final, and four times in the game to decide third and fourth place.

★ ★ ★

Of the sixteen nations appearing in the final stages of the competition, Brazil have the best record. They have won nineteen of their twenty-nine games with a percentage of 74.1. They are closely followed by Uruguay (71.9 per cent) and Italy (70.6 per cent).

No substitutes are allowed in World Cup games and this is the first World Cup competition played under the F.I.F.A. rules which set out to outlaw the use of players of naturalised nationality.

★ ★ ★

Six of the sixteen finalists have red as their first-choice colour—Chile, Hungary, North Korea, Russia, Spain, and Switzerland. The other colours are: Argentina—blue and white stripes; Brazil—yellow and green; Bulgaria—white; England—white; France—blue; Italy—blue; Mexico—green; Portugal—white; Uruguay—sky blue; West Germany—white. When two countries with the same colours are drawn against each other F.I.F.A. will decide which team has to change.

★ ★ ★

Carbajal, the Mexican goalkeeper, may have set up an unbeatable record by appearing in every post-war World Cup competition, but his appearances have not been crowned with success. He has played ten World Cup games and been on the winning side just once—against Czechoslovakia in 1962.

RADIO TIMES July 28, 1966

JULY 30

TV SATURDAY

WORLD CUP GRANDSTAND 12.0 to 5.20

INTRODUCED BY DAVID COLEMAN
DIRECT FROM WEMBLEY

The World Cup Final

BBC outside broadcast cameras and commentary teams cover the whole of today's great occasion at the Empire Stadium, Wembley, to decide the world football champions of 1966

12.0 WORLD CUP FINAL PREVIEW
David Coleman with latest news of the teams and match conditions

12.30 THE WEMBLEY SCENE
David Coleman, with Johnny Haynes, Danny Blanchflower, Tommy Docherty, and Jimmy Hill, joins the crowds at Wembley and looks forward to the match

1.30 HOW THEY GOT THERE
Kenneth Wolstenholme introduces film of the two teams in action on their way to the Wembley final

1.45 PEOPLE AT THE MATCH
David Coleman talks to some of the personalities at today's match, including the winners of the Grandstand World Football Team contest

1.55 MEET THE TEAMS
Film of the twenty-two players who take part in the Final

2.10 INSIDE WEMBLEY
Band of the Royal Marines, Portsmouth Group, conducted by Captain P. A. G. Sumner, L.R.A.M., A.R.C., R.M., Director of Music

2.50 PRESENTATION OF THE TEAMS

● **3.0 KICK OFF** Commentator, Kenneth Wolstenholme

3.45 HALF TIME
Marching display by the Royal Marines, Portsmouth Group

● **3.55 SECOND HALF**

4.45 PRESENTATION OF THE JULES RIMET TROPHY
to the World Champions of 1966

4.50 THE WINNERS
The men of the match and an expert view of the new champions by the Grandstand team of experts
Television presentation by Alec Weeks, Alan Mouncer, and Richard Tilling

---

CRICKET: Glamorgan v. West Indies
At intervals during the afternoon, visits to Swansea for the first day of this match in which the tourists play their last game before resuming the Test series against England. Commentators, Peter West, Brian Johnston, Wilfred Wooller, and Richie Benaud
Television presentation by Dewi Griffiths

Programme editors, Lawrie Higgins and Alan Hart
Executive producers, Alan Chivers and Bryan Cowgill

BBC-1

11.55 a.m.
NOTICE BOARD
Public Service announcements

12.0
WORLD CUP GRANDSTAND
See panel
In the event of extra time being played GRANDSTAND will be extended to cover the end of the match and the victory scenes

5.20
LAUREL AND HARDY
A new selection of short films by two of the world's great laughter-makers
This week:
County Hospital
A Hal Roach film
Directed by James Parrott
Ollie is in hospital with his leg in plaster. A visit from Stanley does not exactly speed his recovery!

5.40
JUKE BOX JURY
A new disc—a Hit or a Miss? Comments and opinions on the latest pop releases
This week's panel:
Dave Cash
Joy Marshall
Jackie Stewart
Susan Hampshire
In the chair, David Jacobs
Programme devised by Peter Potter
Presentation, Terry Henebery

6.5
THE NEWS
and
THE WEATHER

BBC-2

3.30 p.m.-5.0
THE GREAT DAN PATCH
starring
DENNIS O'KEEFE
GAIL RUSSELL
with
Ruth Warrick
Directed by Joe Newman
David Palmer............DENNIS O'KEEFE
Cissy......................GAIL RUSSELL
Ruth......................RUTH WARRICK
Aunt Kitty........CHARLOTTE GREENWOOD
Pop........................HENRY HULL
Jed....................ARTHUR HUNNICUTT
Ben.........................JOHN HOYT
The life and times of a spectacular horse which broke all American championship pacing records in the early 1900s.

6.15
QUICK BEFORE THEY CATCH US
with
TEDDY GREEN
as Johnny
PAMELA FRANKLIN
as Kate
DAVID GRIFFIN
as Mark
and
Colin Bell
as Don
Colin Douglas
as Mr. Lane
☆
Season of the Skylark
by JACK TREVOR STORY
featuring
Campbell Singer, John Gill
Betty Baskcomb, Jean St. Clair
4: A fight with the police... lightning rescue... and the truth at last.
Det.-Inspector Jugg..........HUGH CROSS
Magnus......................JOHN GILL
Sailor......................RIC FELGATE
Captain Happy..........CAMPBELL SINGER
Agnes....................JEAN ST. CLAIR
Lolita..................MADELEINE MILLS
Mum....................BETTY BASKCOMB
Harbour Master....DOUGLAS BLACKWELL
Duty Officer.........GEOFFREY ALEXANDER
P.C. Bates................DIXON ADAMS
Cecile.................BETTINE LE BEAU
Mrs. Pilsworth............BETTY ENGLAND
Theme song by MONTY NORMAN
Designer, Barry Newbery
Producer, WILLIAM STERLING
† Directed by MORRIS BARRY

6.40
THE MUNSTERS
A comedy film series featuring a friendly family of well-known weirdies
starring
FRED GWYNNE
as Herman Munster
YVONNE DE CARLO
as Lily Munster
and
AL LEWIS
as Grandpa
with
Pat Priest, Butch Patrick
☆
Don't Bank on Herman
... his bank can't take it!

7.5
THE DICK VAN DYKE SHOW
A comedy film series featuring the hilarious adventures of a happy-go-lucky scriptwriter and his family
starring
DICK VAN DYKE
with
Mary Tyler Moore
Morey Amsterdam
Rose Marie, Larry Mathews
☆
Odd But True
... there's more to a bell than a clapper!

* Approximate time
† BBC recording

Thursday

Radio Times — The Sixties 1966

SPORTS REVIEW OF THE YEAR
BBC-1 at 9.30

Tonight you have a chance to relive some of the great moments of a year rich in vivid sporting memories. You can also find out whom you have chosen as Sportsview Personality of 1966 when the trophy is presented before an invited audience of sports stars at the BBC Television Theatre. As well you can see the presentation of two other awards — to the Team of the Year and the Outstanding Sports star from Overseas

Bobby McGregor—one of the sporting stars you can see in action tonight

Gary Sobers—Captain of the West Indies cricket team

Cassius Clay (Muhammad Ali) in action against Cleveland Williams

Billie-Jean King and Manuel Santana—two enormously popular Wimbledon winners

Walter McGowan— World Flyweight Champion

Lynn Davies— European Long Jump Champion

Jack Brabham—World Champion Driver, in a car he built himself

A surprise in the Grand National (50-1 winner) clears the final f...

Tonight on BBC-1
SPORTS REVIEW OF 1966
FEATURING THE
Sportsview Personality of the Year
The World Cup Champions
AND
Britain's Other Champions in 1966

ENGLAND HEROES
On 15 December, the World Cup winners were guests of honour at the BBC and the Sportsview Personality of the Year trophy was awarded — with no surprise — to England captain Bobby Moore

9.30
SPORTS REVIEW OF 1966
Introduced by **Frank Bough**
featuring the
SPORTSVIEW PERSONALITY OF THE YEAR

Tonight's gala *Sportsview* comes from the stage of the BBC Television Theatre in London, before an audience of more than 300 sporting personalities
featuring
The World Cup Champions
Meet...
England's winning team in person with **David Coleman**
and see again the highlights of the World Cup

Britain's other champions in 1966 including:
**Jack Brabham, Lynn Davies
Beryl Burton, Walter McGowan
Barry Briggs**
and the highlights of the past twelve months
THE EMPIRE GAMES
THE EUROPEAN GAMES
THE GRAND NATIONAL
THE WEST INDIAN TEST SERIES
THE WORLD HEAVYWEIGHT CHAMPIONSHIP
WIMBLEDON
JIM RYUN'S WORLD MILE RECORD
and action from a dozen sports
and announcing the awards to:
The Team of the Year
The Outstanding Sports Star from Overseas
and, for Britain
The Sportsview Personality of 1966
who receives the trophy from
Denis Howell, M.P.
Minister with special responsibility for Sport
Designer, Paul Munting
Produced by RICHARD TILLING
Editor, ALAN HART

See page 45

Carol White and Ray Brooks star in THE WEDNESDAY PLAY

'The outcry was extraordinary'

Cathy Come Home was a harrowing, revolutionary BBC drama, which is highly revered and, sadly, still relevant today. Producer Tony Garnett introduced the play in *Radio Times* (right) in 1966, while its writer Jeremy Sandford (opposite page) spoke of its impact in *RT* in 1968. Now, in 2022, its director **Ken Loach** reflects on their film's enduring legacy…

"We were lucky. We produced dramas for The Wednesday Play with a brief to be contemporary and challenging. Instead of working in the studio, we wanted to be outside on the streets with a small hand-held camera. With reluctance, the BBC agreed. *Cathy* was the first film we made.

"Homelessness was a national scandal. Families with children were given emergency accommodation that was very basic and, for those who could not move on, it was so bad it felt like a punishment for being poor. Fathers were turned away; only mothers and children were housed. It was shameful to be homeless. *Cathy Come Home* told the story of one such family. Carol White and Ray Brooks were heartbreaking as the young couple, and Carol's own two boys were their children. In the final scene, with Cathy looking for shelter for the night, her children were taken by social workers.

"We knew we were on to something, but the outcry after the broadcast was extraordinary. How could this happen in the Britain of those days? The press took up the story, there were questions in Parliament and we went to see the housing minister. There was one change – husbands were allowed to stay in temporary accommodation with their families. But nothing fundamental was changed. There's a surprise!

"And now? Homelessness is worse than ever. The consequences for all in this plight can be devastating, but children suffer the most. Housing is seen as a commodity, and the market has failed the people.

"Again, we were lucky – only answerable to a supportive and fearless Head of Drama, Sydney Newman. Now directors complain of micro-management and over-zealous supervision across all the channels. Cathy is still on the streets, but her story may not be told with the raw savagery it deserves."

CATHY COME HOME

'*I reckon it's just us now. Just you and me. Have some kids, eh Cath?*'
'*I'd like that.*'

1
9.5

CATHY is blonde and attractive with an open, determined face. Just up from the country and in the big city she meets Reg and falls for him. He is so easy-going and relaxed and full of laughs. She dreams of settling down, building a home and having some babies. A natural thing to want, one might think, and something we all have a right to look forward to.

Just a simple love story. But things don't turn out for her quite like that. Events cruelly overtake her and Reg—and later their children. They begin a journey through Britain, but it is a Britain many of us have never seen. What happens to them we may scarcely believe. But it is happening now, and is likely to go on happening to lots of people for a long time.

Everything in tonight's play the author Jeremy Sandford has seen with his own eyes. It is something he feels deeply and his passion and his anger leap out at us from this story of two human beings trying to make a home for themselves and their children. Trying, with humour and love and courage, to live decent lives and keep their self-respect.

Cathy Come Home is directed by Kenneth Loach, whose outstanding contributions to 'The Wednesday Play' last year included *Three Clear Sundays* and *Up the Junction*. Carol White and Ray Brooks play the young people.
TONY GARNETT

POINTS FROM THE POST

Cathy Come Home

Many congratulations to BBC-1 for unquestionably the most realistic documentary drama ever presented in *Cathy Come Home*, and for the splendid follow-up discussion on BBC-2 in *Late Night Line-Up*.

At last! Authentic, factual, unambiguous, meticulous in detail, brilliant in presentation, a superb television report on a most urgent problem of today.

Without doubt, a real TV breakthrough from the morass of trivial, fictional miasma we have had for years.

Please give us more realism like this to start controversy. — *R. E. Doherty, Manchester, 20.*

We live in a tatty, prefabricated house in this small unadventurous town of the Midlands. We thought ourselves as being lower working class. That was until we saw *Cathy Come Home*. Now our opinions have changed.

May I offer my sincere thanks to all concerned for this superb reminder that the grass is certainly greener *this* side of the hill. — *S. E. Higley, Nuneaton.*

We are frustrated and irritated when, after watching a good programme such as BBC-1's *Cathy Come Home*, we are told it is to be discussed later on BBC-2.

Surely those of us who cannot yet receive or perhaps afford BBC-2 should not be subjected to this hardship?

Besides, a large percentage of the people who have BBC-2 are likely to have been on that channel and not to have seen the programme to be discussed in *Late Night Line-Up*. — *R. S. Snow, Shrewsbury.*

We are receiving an unusually heavy post on this play. Almost without exception the letters express praise for it—and distress at the plight of the homeless it revealed so movingly. — *Editor.*

CATHY HIT HOME

The *Radio Times* mailbag was inundated with praise for *Cathy Come Home*. The acclaimed film was reshown in January 1967, November 1968 and several more times in subsequent decades

---

Radio Times
The Sixties 1966

CATHY? TO BRITAIN'S SHAME, THERE ARE STILL TOO MANY LIKE HER

JEREMY SANDFORD writes about his much-discussed Cathy Come Home which is being given another showing as The Wednesday Play

 WED 9.10

If any writer ever hoped that an idea of his would be accepted by the public as valid and taken to their hearts, then he would have hoped for the reaction that has followed my *Cathy Come Home*.

If any writer ever hoped that what he wrote would be embodied in flesh and blood with power, accuracy, beauty, then he would have hoped for a director like Ken Loach, and a performance such as Carol White's.

And if ever a writer hoped that, in however small a way, what he wrote would result in changes in the manner that his country was run, then that writer would be me. Because there have been changes, small but none the less important, which, it might not be too much to believe, were the result of *Cathy*.

I wrote *Cathy* in bitterness and anger because I had seen happening to a girl, a neighbour of mine, and her children, the things that happened to Cathy. Later I learned that this sort of thing was happening not only to her—but to thousands of others, and this increased my sorrow and my anger.

I wrote it late in 1963 and for three years I could find no organisation prepared to put it on. Then *Cathy* was bought by Tony Garnett for the BBC and there were hundreds of letters at the time of that first showing, thanking me that at last the truth had been told about one area of life as it really is in Britain.

The facts of *Cathy* have often been questioned but, I claim, cannot be faulted. They are true. Some of the things shown in the film happen more rarely than others. The taking of children from their parents, as shown at the end of the film, doesn't often happen by force, but it *does* happen sometimes that parents fight for their children. With 5,000 children in care for no other reason than that their parents can find no home for them, it would be surprising if it didn't.

And I might note here that since *Cathy*, the number of these children has increased by one whole thousand from the figure of 4,000 given in the film.

Most of the other conditions shown in *Cathy* are still all too painfully with us. The desolate squalor of many caravan sites, the housing lists that run into thousands, the millions of people living in slum conditions, the overcrowding—there has been little improvement here.

Numbers in hostels for the homeless have risen from 12,500 at the time of the film to 15,000 now.

The eviction, the fire, life in the slum, all these scenes in *Cathy* were modelled on life.

So, too, were those scenes in which Cathy is trying to sleep out with her family in ruined buildings, in a tent, anything rather than having to face the humiliation of going into public care.

It has been said that all the things that happened to Cathy could not have happened to one person.

This is false. The odysseys of those who end up in Britain's Homes for the Homeless are often far more complicated than those undertaken by Cathy.

I know, because I have spoken with many of them. Since *Cathy*, Shelter has been formed, a national campaign to keep alive that compassion and responsible concern for the victims of Britain's housing situation which *Cathy* may have helped to arouse. And we are building more houses. But, I would say, still not fast enough. Officials may not, I would say, always get the most accurate picture since they see members of Britain's homeless in a tense atmosphere, across a desk.

But to talk with Britain's real-life Cathys, as I have done, face to face and heart to heart —might end not in an official document but in a play like *Cathy*.

Radio Times
The Sixties 1966

TILL DEATH US DO PART

A new comedy series by Johnny Speight

1
7.30

THE series beginning tonight is yet another 'spin-off' from BBC-1's highly successful *Comedy Playhouse*. The star of the series is the script, written by Johnny Speight, who is one of the country's top comedy writers. He wrote the first Eric Sykes-Hattie Jacques series, and has just completed his tenth year of writing for Arthur Haynes.

Till Death Us Do Part is set at the far eastern end of Wapping High Street in London's dockland.

The cast is headed by **Warren Mitchell**, who plays the father—Alf Garnett. He is working class, skilled at his trade, three generations behind the times, and is well endowed with most natural human failings. He is narrow-minded, prejudiced, selfish, greedy, cowardly, and very, very proud of himself. He is a self-confessed expert on any subject. He is also a Tory and a Monarchist, but has never forgiven Edward Heath for trying to get us into the Common Market. It need hardly be said, therefore, that Harold Wilson and the Labour Party are utterly wrong as far as he is concerned. The same also goes for General de Gaulle, the Russians, the Chinese— all foreigners—and the gentleman who is in charge of Big Ben 'because the clock's always wrong . . .'

But what wounds Alf's permanently hurt pride most is his young son-in-law Mike (played by **Anthony Booth**). Young, good-looking, virile, strictly of this new generation which rejects all the lovely traditional shibboleths in which Britain has wallowed since Queen Victoria, he tears down every belief that the older man depends upon.

Dandy Nichols plays Else, Alf Garnett's wife, who is a pale echo of her old man, and is vaguely worried as well—by the price of eggs and the fact that the weather hasn't been so good since Labour got in.

There is but one beautiful flower growing in the middle of this compost heap—the Garnetts' daughter Rita (played by **Una Stubbs**). Pretty as a picture, she has no neuroses and is utterly happy as befits a bride of eight weeks.

DENNIS MAIN WILSON

ALF WIT

Dennis Main Wilson was one of the most influential producers in BBC comedy, having nurtured the Goons, Tony Hancock and Eric Sykes. Writing for *RT* in 1966, he introduced Johnny Speight's radical sitcom focused on the bigoted Alf Garnett. Below: Don Smith photographed the four stars of *Till Death* – Anthony Booth, Una Stubbs, Warren Mitchell and Dandy Nichols

5-3-65

DAVID ATTENBOROUGH IS NEW CHIEF OF B.B.C. - 2..

It was announced yesterday that the post of Chief of B.B.C. 2 - had been given to DAVID ATTENBOROUGH 38 year old brother of film actor Richard Attenborough. The job was offered to him by HUW WELDON the new Chief of B.B.C. television programmes - after it had been refused by Donald Baverstock..

RADIO TIMES June 9, 1966

A TRULY NATIONAL NETWORK

A progress report by DAVID ATTENBOROUGH Controller, BBC-2

HE'S A NATURAL

In the mid 1960s, naturalist David Attenborough assumed a new role when he took control of BBC2. Pictured (above) in 1965, he updated *RT* readers on the network's progress in 1966 (right). During his stewardship, he oversaw the launch of colour television on BBC2, then became the BBC's Director of Programmes in 1969. In 1972, he returned to filming with the BBC's Natural History Unit

A NEW television network has a choice to make. It can either show variations of programmes that have already proved their success and popularity on other networks; or it can try to create something new. By finding fresh faces, by putting familiar ones in different settings, most of all by tackling subjects that other television networks have largely ignored, it can bring new excitements and pleasures to television viewing.

BBC-2 has taken the second alternative. Its programmes cover golf and archaeology; science-fiction and Rugby League; jazz, motoring, and opera; foreign films and folk music. It introduced *The Likely Lads* and *Not Only . . . But Also*. It has devised new styles of presentation in music, documentary, and children's programmes.

Novelty, however, is not our only objective. We also try to arrange our schedules so that each programme differs as widely as possible in style and content from the programme being shown simultaneously on BBC-1. The result is that viewers, for the first time, have carefully planned alternatives in their evening's entertainment. *The Danny Kaye Show*, for example, is paired with *Panorama*, *Thirty-Minute Theatre* with *Songs for the Times*, *The Brothers Karamazov* serial with *Sportsview*.

Two years ago BBC-2 could be seen only by a restricted number of people in the London area. Next month, when our new transmitters in Scotland and Yorkshire officially open, our programmes will be within the reach of over half Britain. BBC-2 in fact will have become a truly national network.

In its short life so far the network has been attacked and flattered, criticised and praised. Today the commonest complaint is from viewers who feel frustrated because many of BBC-2's programmes are not shown on BBC-1. BBC-1's policy, however, has not changed since the arrival of the new network and it could find room for BBC-2's programmes only by displacing its own established favourites. A quart, unhappily, will never go into a pint pot. One writer asked angrily: 'What is the BBC trying to do— deliberately force people to watch BBC-2?'

If we are forcing people to watch us by putting on the best, the most exciting and adventurous programmes that we know how, then I suppose we must plead guilty.

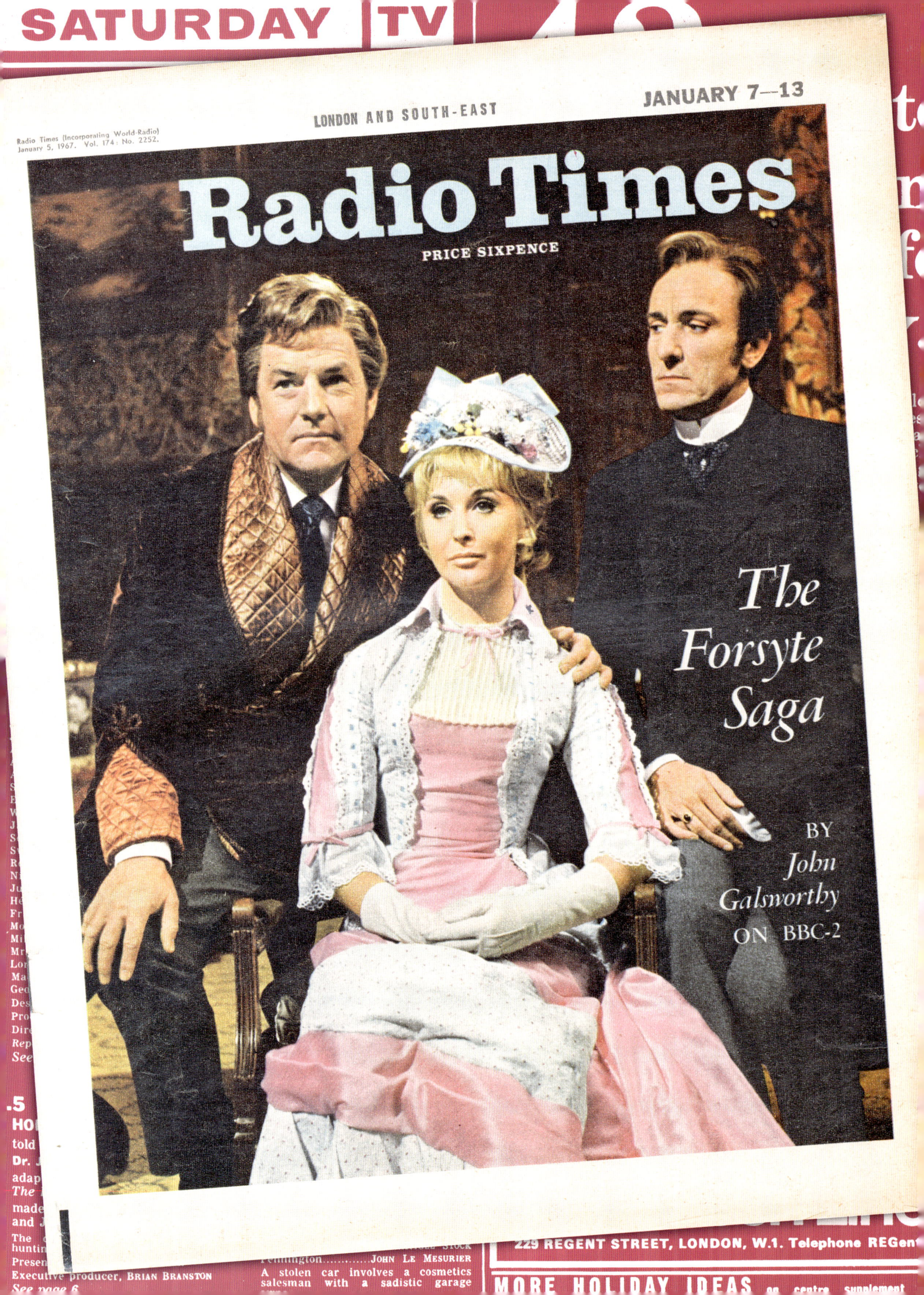
SATURDAY TV
Radio Times (Incorporating World-Radio) January 5, 1967. Vol. 174: No. 2252.
LONDON AND SOUTH-EAST
JANUARY 7—13
Radio Times
PRICE SIXPENCE
The Forsyte Saga
BY John Galsworthy ON BBC-2
Executive producer, BRIAN BRANSTON
See page 6
Pennington.............JOHN LE MESURIER
A stolen car involves a cosmetics salesman with a sadistic garage
229 REGENT STREET, LONDON, W.1. Telephone REGent
MORE HOLIDAY IDEAS

1967
THE FORSYTE SAGA

RADIO TIMES January 5, 1967

Galsworthy's story of a prosperous English family told in twenty-six parts—Saturdays on BBC-2. The Forsytes' watchword is Respectability, Property its God; but Beauty and Passion steal into the family citadel—destroying its solidarity, setting husband against wife, father against son

Addictive viewing

The Forsyte Saga was one of the last prestigious BBC drama series to be made in black-and-white. Starring Kenneth More, Nyree Dawn Porter and Eric Porter (pictured on the *RT* cover, opposite page), it followed the affairs of an upper middle-class family across many decades from 1879 to 1926, and sprawled over 26 weeks on BBC2 in 1967.

The series was highly praised, but it was a much-requested repeat on BBC1 in 1968/69 that truly captivated the nation – with 18 million tuning in. There were reports of pubs closing early across the land and church services being retimed to accommodate *Forsyte* fans.

Don Smith joined *Radio Times* full time as its staff photographer during the making of the *Saga* in spring 1967. Although he wasn't assigned to do so, he continued to document each episode, as he explained in 2015. "Sometimes these shows were done a year in advance and none of the *RT* people would know anything about them. Often I'd think, 'God, this is a good show. It's going to catch on,' so I'd make a point of shooting it whenever I could."

In the event, Smith was on set for 25 of the 26 instalments, and hundreds of his *Forsyte Saga* images are now preserved in the *RT* archive.

SAGA ON CAMERA

Above: a rare colour shot of Emily Forsyte (Fanny Rowe), her son-in-law Monty (Terence Alexander) and daughter Winifred (Margaret Tyzack)

Left: Jo Forsyte (Kenneth More) and his soon-to-be third wife Irene (Nyree Dawn Porter) in episode 11

8.15
THE FORSYTE SAGA
by JOHN GALSWORTHY
dramatised by DONALD WILSON
starring
KENNETH MORE
ERIC PORTER
PART 1: A Family Festival
Jo .... KENNETH MORE
Jolyon .... JOSEPH O'CONOR
Aunt Ann .... FAY COMPTON
Aunt Juley .... NORA NICHOLSON
Aunt Hester .... NORA SWINBURNE
Smither .... MAGGIE JONES
Emily .... FANNY ROWE
Winifred .... MARGARET TYZACK
James .... JOHN WELSH
Soames .... ERIC PORTER
Swithin .... GEORGE WOODBRIDGE
Roger .... A. J. BROWN
Nicholas .... KYNASTON REEVES
June .... SUSAN PENNICK
Hélène .... LANA MORRIS
Frances .... URSULA HOWELLS
Monty .... TERENCE ALEXANDER
Millie .... DEDDIE DAVIES
Mrs. Heron .... JENNY LAIRD
Lomax .... CAMPBELL

75

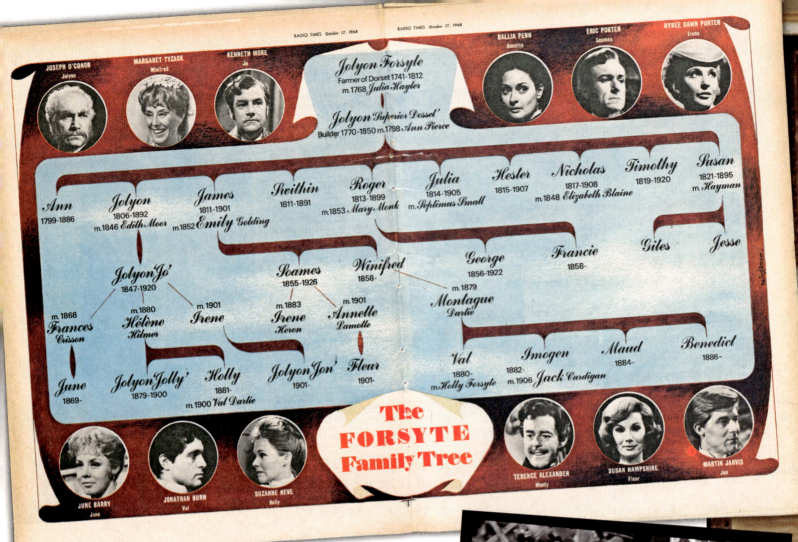

'I played Fleur as a monster'

Midway into *The Forsyte Saga*, the storyline jumped ahead several years with **Susan Hampshire** and Martin Jarvis injecting some youth as lovelorn Fleur and Jon Forsyte. How was it coming into such a prestigious drama halfway into the run?

"Martin and I were very lucky," Hampshire tells *RT* in 2022. "We'd never met before and were thrown into a romantic story, filming in the countryside, so we formed a bond between ourselves as friends and actors and with the director, James Cellan Jones.

"Then when we met the cast, I was again lucky. Eric Porter liked working with me. I mean, what a blessing! He played my father [Soames]. Maggie Tyzack [Aunt Winifred] was also very kind and said, 'I'm so pleased you aren't trying to play this part for sympathy.' So I played Fleur as the monster she was, a hugely interesting human being. Playing somebody who's not nice is much more rewarding. Playing a nice person is such hard work and you get no credit for it."

She recalls the tight production schedule of television drama in those days. "I've a feeling we had two weeks' rehearsal then two days in the studio. But the videotape couldn't be cut. You had to do all the quick changes as though you were in a play and run from one set to another. It was literally like doing it live.

Demanding but very enjoyable."

Back then she also appreciated being able to refer back to John Galsworthy's books. "You had more information and detail than you would with just the script. The scriptwriter has the difficult task of concertina-ing a novel or a series of novels. But it's easier to take a mediocre book and turn it into a brilliantly exciting television series than to adapt a great classic like *War and Peace* because the expectation is completely different and the human story is easier to bring to life."

As for the mass appeal of the *Saga*: "It was phenomenal. Everyone knows about the church services having to change their times because people wanted to get home in time to watch it. Every country in the world, including Russia, loved it. Suddenly one was on the cover of *Paris Match* when it was shown in France. Nicholas Pennell [who played Fleur's husband Michael] and I were invited to Sweden by Ingmar Bergman. All the roads were lined from the airport to Stockholm. We went to a stadium with 30,000 people. It was like being the Beatles."

MEETINGS
Right: Jon (Martin Jarvis) falls for Fleur (Susan Hampshire) in episode 13
Below: Soames (Eric Porter) shares his dark past with daughter Fleur in episode 15

POINTS FROM THE POST

They Watch It Twice

BBC-2's *The Forsyte Saga* is the most wonderful thing that has happened on television.

I watch it spellbound on Saturdays—and again on Tuesdays. This, to me, is proof of an excellent production and cast.

I would like to suggest an equally challenging and dramatic assignment for Donald Wilson when the *Saga* is finished: *The Herries Chronicle*, by Hugh Walpole.—(Mrs.) M. Parry, Manchester.

I MUST say how much my family and I enjoy *The Forsyte Saga*; we watch it twice a week.

The acting is superb, the story fascinating—it's the very best show on BBC at this time.

May there be many more series to follow like this, which really makes television worth watching.—(Mrs.) M. C. Bonsall, Ventnor.

Compulsive Viewing

Now that *The Forsyte Saga* on BBC-2 is getting into its stride may I say what compulsive viewing this serial is?

All the characters who etched such a firm place in my memory from many years ago are coming magically to life.

Add to this the gorgeous dresses (impossible to think of any of these creatures in a mini-skirt!) and John Galsworthy's amazing insight into the human heart, especially the female variety, and you have a surefire winner.

I'm glad we've got BBC-2.—(Mrs.) C. Kennard, Harrow

The Saga

A HEARTFELT 'thank you' for the wonderful serialisation on BBC-2 of *The Forsyte Saga*.

Everyone concerned in the production should be congratulated and thanked for providing first-class entertainment.

What a joy it has been to savour this for six whole months!—(Mr. and Mrs.) J. Widdop, Barrowford, Lancs.

A flood of eulogies from readers (whom we thank here), signalising the final instalment of the *Saga*. A radio version in forty-eight parts begins in the Home Service on July 25—EDITOR

THE LAST FORSYTES

On 9 June 1967, the cast gathered for a formal family portrait taken by *RT*'s Don Smith during rehearsals for the 25th and penultimate episode. By this stage many actors were wearing ageing make-up. Left to right, the women: June (June Barry), Winifred (Margaret Tyzack), Fleur (Susan Hampshire), Irene (Nyree Dawn Porter), Holly (Suzanne Neve) and Anne (Karin Fernald). The men: Sir Lawrence (Cyril Luckham), Michael (Nicholas Pennell), Soames (Eric Porter), Jon (Martin Jarvis) and Val (Jonathan Burn)

Baftas were awarded to the series and Eric Porter in 1968

The End of the Saga
Producer Donald Wilson writes:

9.55

THIS evening, after six months on the air, *The Forsyte Saga* comes to its conclusion with the final episode, which we have called 'Swan Song,' the title of the last of Galsworthy's six novels. For those who have worked on the serial for so many months it will be an occasion mixed with relief and regret.

Relief at a long and arduous task at last complete; regret because during over a year of filming, rehearsals, and recordings, we have become a family nearly as close-knit as the Forsytes themselves, though without, I am happy to report, their distressing habit of scratching out each others eyes. But the comparison should not be pressed too hard. We have been, after all, only a body of carefully selected artists and technicians bound to a common purpose for a while, and now dispersed. New employment and new challenges await us; new relationships, too, and more than likely these will be as rewarding as those we now sever. And yet, sentiment apart, the regret persists.

Because, from the first reading of the first script a remarkable sense of harmony has prevailed between us all, a close harmony that no disagreement has been able to flaw. And this is a splendid thing in the world of drama, where the pressures between producer, director, actor, and technician can so often result in disunity. But when it happens, work becomes a delight instead of just another chore, and then perhaps some of our own excitement and pleasure rubs off, so to speak, upon the screen and is communicated to the viewer.

So, as the last act of this long tale is played tonight, we, who have so much enjoyed the telling of it, would like to believe that you, our audience, will also feel a pang of regret at reading 'The End.'

77

Radio Times
The Sixties 1967

RADIO 1/2/3/4

SWINGING AND NEW

BBC Radio underwent a radical shake-up on 30 September 1967. Frank Gillard, the executive in charge, explained the changes to the existing networks in *Radio Times* (below), and ushered in Radio 1, the brand-new BBC station dedicated to pop. *RT* marked the occasion with a special cover shoot and a model in a paper dress — held taut with a line of thread to display the 247 frequency. These rare alternative shots have only just come to light

SEPTEMBER 30, 1967, will be a milestone day for BBC Radio. On that date the Light Programme will split into two, and a new Radio network will come into operation. It will provide a day-long popular music service for listeners who want bright, cheerful, informal, musical entertainment uninterrupted by spoken word items. Meanwhile the old, traditional Light, which has proved its enduring popularity by the way in which it has successfully withstood keen competition from offshore stations in recent years, will still be available on the alternative channel.

A new network requires a name, and to find the right one is no easy matter. A choice based on current circumstances does not necessarily have any lasting meaning. Take 'Home Service' for example. This was a good name in 1939 when the Programme was introduced at the outbreak of war. The BBC at that time had only two services in English, one for listeners in this country and one for listeners abroad. To call one 'Home' and the other 'Overseas' was sensible. But, apart from convention which younger generations do not always understand or value, 'Home Service' has little real meaning as a title for one particular programme in the 1960s when the BBC is offering three or four networks to the listener at home. For this and other reasons, the BBC has decided that with the introduction of this additional popular music service the time has come to review the names of all its Radio networks.

The new names must be straightforward, and easily understood and memorised. Once engraved on the dials of millions of radio receivers they cannot easily be changed. So the decisions now being taken need to be flexible, and adaptable to unforeseeable circumstances.

In the light of these considerations the simplest solution seems to be the best. The four networks will simply be called Radio 1, Radio 2, Radio 3, and Radio 4. RADIO TIMES, newspaper, and microphone announcements will carry the new identifications from September 30 onwards. But to avoid confusion, and to help listeners to become accustomed gradually to these developments, the old names will be kept in use along with the new ones for some considerable time. The two will run together for at least a couple of years until the changes have been widely understood and accepted.

The new popular music service will be introduced as **Radio 1**, while the Light Programme will in due course become **Radio 2**, and the Home Service, with its customary Regional variations, will eventually be known as **Radio 4**. Until the time comes for the names 'Home Service' and 'Light Programme' to disappear altogether, the announcers will be using such network identification phrases as 'This is the Home Service on Radio 4,' or 'On Radio 2 the Light Programme presents . . .' The Regions will adapt their announcements as they wish— perhaps in such forms as 'This is Radio 4 from the North,' or 'This is Scotland on Radio 4.' It is one of the merits of the new system that it combines well with the old in this way, and permits change to take place gradually.

So far I have said nothing about **Radio 3**. It is a special case, since it will be the new name of the Third Network and will, of course, continue to provide the same services. This

network, unlike the others, carries not one Programme but four—at different times on familiar days. The four are: The Music Programme, Study Session, **The Third Programme**, and Sports Service. Since they are the components of a single network, these four Programmes will retain their titles, but the announcers will be giving reminders that they **are broadcast on the Radio 3 network.**

Why are the numbers allocated in this order, with the **Home Service,** by long tradition the BBC's central Radio Programme, apparently at the bottom of the list? Two factors were inescapable in the interests **of** clarity and simplicity: (a) the two Light **services had to** be given consecutive numbering; **(b) everything** at present associated with the **Third Network** had to be kept on Radio 3. So inescapably the Home Service had to become Radio 4. **This is** the only significance of the numbering sequence. No upgrading or downgrading is implied. The numerals in no way denote priorities.

'Home Service' has **been with us for** twenty-eight years, '**Light Programme**' for twenty-two. These **names will be around for** quite a **while yet before the time comes for** final **retirement with honour.** The titles which **succeed them may well endure for decades. By** their nature they could last indefinitely. We commend them, and the brand new Radio One network which comes with them, as important and historic developments in BBC broadcasting.

FRANK GILLARD,
Director of Radio, BBC
Wavelengths and frequencies for Radio 1 and Radio 2 will be set out in full in Radio Times issue dated September 23

79

RIGHT TONE
On Saturday 30 September 1967, Tony Blackburn got Radio 1 off to a groovy start with the Move's *Flowers in the Rain* as his first record. He hosted the breakfast show six mornings a week until 1973 and remains a fixture on BBC Radio to this day

'The 60s was the best decade ever'

"I say it every week on *Sounds of the 60s*, but it *was* the best decade ever," **Tony Blackburn** tells *RT* in 2022. He has now been hosting the Radio 2 show for five years but, for many listeners, he's personified the sound of the 1960s since launching Radio 1 back in 1967 – and even before that DJ-ing on the pirate radio ships. "From 1964, I spent three years out on the North Sea with Radio Caroline, then a year with Big L Radio London, before opening up Radio 1. So it was quite an eventful decade."

For Blackburn, it's always been about the music. "I thought it was fantastic. There was Beatlemania, the Rolling Stones and Tom Jones – his voice is still as great today as it was in the 60s. Dusty Springfield was one of the best soul singers in this country. I've always had a love of black soul music, particularly Motown and Philadelphia, so Diana Ross and the Supremes, Marvin Gaye and Stevie Wonder – those were my real favourites. Great artists creating great songs.

"I mean, not every song that came out was good, but they just had a knack in the 60s of writing short, catchy songs – like *Downtown* with Petula Clark, *Reach Out I'll Be There* by the Four Tops, and the Supremes' hits *In and Out of Love* and *Stop! In the Name of Love*. The interesting thing is when Diana Ross was at the Glastonbury Festival this summer, even the youngsters in the audience all knew her songs."

When the BBC lured a 24-year-old Blackburn away from the pirate ships, he was tried out initially for two months on the Light Programme. "I went in to do the *Midday Spin* and the producer said, 'Can I have your script?' I said, 'Well, I've never had a script. I ad-lib.' They weren't used to that at the old-fashioned BBC, so he said – it was very funny – 'Would you mind coming in an hour before the programme anyway? Otherwise I have to cancel the doughnuts and coffee.'"

After that strange introduction, Blackburn was delighted to be given free rein for the Radio 1 launch on 30 September 1969. "They didn't say, 'Look, we've done it this way for years. You do it our way now.' They said, 'Go ahead and make it sound good.' They gave Kenny Everett and me a lot of freedom and built a self-operating studio, which we all work to now. My producer Tim Blackmore and I put our own playlist together and played proper vinyl records in those days. We brought them over in a box every morning."

He continued a format honed on pirate radio with jingles, witty intros to each track and a smattering of corny jokes. "I was influenced as a youngster – though he wouldn't like me to say it – by Pete Murray on Radio Luxembourg. I liked his style. As for the charts and Top 40, Alan Freeman was very good. Corny jokes, well, I just always find them funny. I decided not to use jokes on *Sounds of the 60s* because it's nice to change your style a bit, but listeners keep sending them in.

"One great thing about the BBC is that they do leave you alone to be a personality. On commercial radio, it's often three tracks in a row and a time check, and you're not allowed to inject personality. For me as a listener, I want to be entertained by people.

"I feel a bit sorry for the kids nowadays because it's a more complicated world. Sometimes you look back and think, 'Was it really as good as that?' and it actually was. The 60s was an amazing era. I absolutely adored it."

RADIO TIMES June 29, 1967

Radio Times
The Sixties 1967

COLOUR comes to BBC-2

YOUR QUESTIONS ANSWERED

When will colour TV start?
The BBC's Colour Television service on BBC-2 will start on December 2. A colour launching period, during which BBC-2 will transmit regularly about five hours of colour programmes each week until the start of the full service, will open on July 1.

Will I be able to receive the colour programmes?
Yes, if you live in an area served by BBC-2. But at the start of the launching period on July 1 colour will be available only from the BBC-2 transmitters at Crystal Palace (serving London and the South East), Sutton Coldfield (the Midlands), Winter Hill (Lancashire), Emley Moor (Yorkshire), Belmont (Lincolnshire), and Rowridge (Southampton area). Colour will become available from other BBC-2 transmitters over the next few months.

Will I need a special set?
Yes. Black-and-white sets cannot be converted to receive colour.

Will I need another aerial?
Yes, unless you already have a BBC-2 aerial installed giving you good reception on this channel.

Can I see black-and-white programmes as well as colour on a colour set?
Yes. Colour receivers will be dual standard and will provide BBC-1, ITV, and BBC-2 in black-and-white as well as the colour programmes.

Will I be able to see the colour programmes in black-and-white on my present set?
Yes. The transmission system employed is what is known as compatible and, providing you have a modern black-and-white set capable of receiving BBC-2, then you will be able to see the colour programme in black-and-white.

Will they be difficult to use?
Most colour receivers to be used in this country will have only one extra control. This control decides the amount of colour in the picture and you will be able to adjust it to suit the lighting conditions in your room and your individual taste.

Will there be many programmes in colour?
Yes. The majority of BBC-2 programmes will be in colour, amounting to between 15 and 25 hours a week.

When will colour be available on BBC-1 and ITV?
It is expected that BBC-1 and ITV colour services will be in operation in London, the Midlands, and the North by the end of 1969.

Will my receiver cover any future transmissions on other channels?
Yes. As future programmes are transmitted the receiver will be capable of receiving them.

Do I need an additional licence for colour?
The Government has announced an additional fee for colour receivers of £5 but it will not be payable until the Postmaster General makes a further announcement.

The answers to these questions have been prepared by the BBC in co-operation with the British Radio Equipment Manufacturers' Association

LAUNCHING COLOUR

By David Attenborough, Controller of BBC-2

THIS week we launch colour. All BBC-2's coverage of the Centre Court at Wimbledon, both live in the afternoon and recorded in the evenings, will be transmitted in colour. So will *One Pair of Eyes* on Saturday, *Impact* on Thursday, and *The Virginian* on Monday. And so will *Late Night Line-Up* every night.

We are showing these launching programmes for three main reasons. First to let viewers see for themselves just how exciting and how technically excellent colour television can be. Second to help television dealers to check on the orientation of aerials and to get experience of handling sets in regular operation. And, third, to enable us to put to its proper use the colour equipment that we now have installed and ready for public transmissions both within our studios and in Outside Broadcasts.

To begin with these programmes can be seen in colour in London, the Midlands, the South, and the North—those areas that receive BBC-2 from the transmitters at Crystal Palace (with four relays), Sutton Coldfield (with three relays), Rowridge, Winter Hill, Emley Moor, and Belmont. In a few months the special circuits linking other BBC-2 transmitters will be completed to bring the colour picture to the whole of the network.

But the launching programmes are only samples. The full service begins on December 2. Then, approximately eighty per cent of BBC-2 will go out in colour, and that will include all types of programmes from light entertainment shows like *International Cabaret* and *The Black and White Minstrels*, to *Theatre 625* and drama serials, film documentaries and quiz shows, sport, operas, and feature films.

Between then and now, the launching programmes will continue every week. Wimbledon will have come to an end, but we have other outside broadcasts in store and other documentary and light entertainment series too. Together these programmes will provide about five hours of colour a week. Many viewers are no doubt waiting to make up their minds about colour until they see it with their own eyes. We offer the launching programmes, with confidence and excitement, as evidence.

THE ARRIVAL OF COLOUR

After years of experimentation, colour television began on BBC2 on 1 July 1967 for viewers in the North, South, Midlands and London, who had the correct TV sets. BBC2 Controller David Attenborough introduced *RT* readers to the new service

---

PROGRAMMES IN COLOUR THIS WEEK

WIMBLEDON
All week, including Match of the Day

ONE PAIR OF EYES
Saturday at 9.25

from the BBC transmitters at
Crystal Palace,
Sutton Coldfield,
Winter Hill, Emley Moor,
Belmont, and Rowridge

THE VIRGINIAN
Monday at 9.55

IMPACT
Thursday at 9.5

LATE NIGHT LINE-UP
every evening

Radio Times
The Sixties 1967

THE WORLD IS WATCHING
On 25 June 1967, *Our World* was an "audacious experiment in international communications" as the USA, USSR, Europe, Canada, Japan and Australia linked up for a live broadcast via satellite. The Beatles were at the forefront of the UK's participation, performing *All You Need Is Love*

...it's the Beatles one of the British contributions to tonight's global entertainment

OUR WORLD

FRIDAY'S RADIO — JUST A MINUTE

7.30 RADIO 4

DAVID HATCH writes:

VERY WELL, I'll come clean—it's a panel game. No, no, hang on; don't go flipping off to the television pages. It'll only take a minute—in fact, *Just a Minute*. In a few seconds I'll give you a subject about which you've got to talk for one minute—without hesitating, going off the point (deviating), or repeating yourself.

Before I begin, get a stopwatch and stand by. O.K.? (Oh, you've got to make it funny, too.) All set?

Your subject is '*Things to do in the bath.*'

Go!... Well, go on, it's easy.

It's only a minute, for heaven's sake, sixty little seconds. You chatter all day about every subject under the sun, I'm sure...

Oh well, never mind. Let's try again. Now really have a go this time. Your subject is '*Chinese restaurants.*' Go!...

[While all those stupid charlies are actually attempting this fatuous exercise, I've just a minute to tell you that our chairman and umpire is **Nicholas Parsons**, that our two male contestants (everyone plays for himself—it's more vicious) are always **Derek Nimmo** and **Clement Freud**. Each week we change our two lady panelists, and in the coming weeks we have **Beryl Reid, Wilma Ewart, Sheila Hancock, Betty Marsden, Isobel Barnett, Aimi MacDonald, Millie, Prunella Scales**, and many others—oh yes, and it's devised by **Ian Messiter** of *Many a Slip* fame.

While those idiots are still waffling on about Chinese restaurants, I can also tell you that each contestant can challenge any other contestant if they feel they are hesitating, deviating or repeating themselves. If the umpire, or indeed the audience, judge too, the challenger has a point, literally, and goes on talking for however many seconds there are left.]

Back into large type, please. Well done, those of you who tried it. Now you'd better go back and read the small print. Always read the small print.

THE REGULAR MINUTE-MEN

WITHOUT HESITATION
Radio 4 favourite *Just a Minute* first aired on 22 December 1967, heralded in *RT* by its original producer David Hatch

Pictured left: long-time host Nicholas Parsons and panellist Derek Nimmo. Kenneth Williams joined the show the following year

Jacqueline

Tonight's film about the remarkable cellist Jacqueline du Pré is introduced by Christopher Nupen

1 10.25

'I heard it on the radio when I was four and although I don't remember the sound I liked it so much apparently that I asked my mother to give me the thing that made that sound. And she did, she gave me a big, big cello which I learnt to play.'

The story seems too simple—too inevitable. But eighteen years later Jacqueline du Pré is among the most successful musicians this country has produced, and if inevitability is not the keynote then a dramatic sense of vocation certainly is.

She wanted nothing so much as to play the cello and the extravagant natural talent was only a start; she had also the character to develop it and the right environment from the beginning.

Her mother, a pianist, bought her the longed-for cello. Then with great flair she wrote tunes for Jacqueline to play, and illustrated them with enticing drawings.

Not that she needed enticing. Her mother recalls a holiday on Dartmoor where it was thought that the cello would hardly be missed and would probably be out of place; so it was left at home. On the third day she found a tearful Jacqueline alone on the moor, and on asking her what was the matter learnt very simply that she missed the cello that much.

There has always been a striking contrast between the simplicity of her everyday personality and the fire of her playing—as if when she plays she is possessed by her own talent. To make the most of this she tells her own story in the film and is seen making music at different ages: with her mother, her teacher William Pleeth, Sir John Barbirolli, and Daniel Barenboim.

She was married to Daniel Barenboim last June; to celebrate the event and provide a climax for the film we invited them to record the Elgar Concerto.

With a spirit that is typical of their music-making they jumped at the chance, chose the New Philharmonia Orchestra, and produced a performance worthy of the occasion.

MUSICAL GENIUS

Cellist Jacqueline du Pré was the toast of the classical scene – her interpretation of the Elgar *Cello Concerto* remains a benchmark to this day. In November 1967, she was profiled in *RT* and on BBC1 by the film-maker Christopher Nupen

A Moving Performance

How can I begin to thank you for the pleasure given in BBC-1's programme on Jacqueline du Pré? To watch the flowering of this young musical genius into a mature cellist by the age of twenty-two was a privilege indeed.

Her performance of the Elgar Cello Concerto with her husband conducting was an experience for which I would willingly pay a year's licence and feel well compensated.

To see on her face such completely unselfconscious absorption in the beauty of the music and to witness the moments of intense joy and oneness with her husband as they shared in the miracle of music-making was indescribably moving.
—(Mrs.) Joan Avis, Exeter.

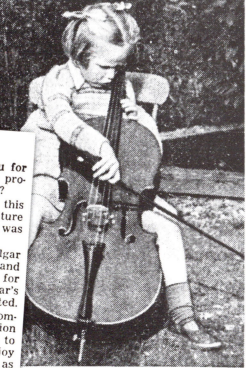

Concentration—Jacqueline as concert-goers see her today and with the 'big, big cello' she played as a child

Radio Times
The Sixties 1967

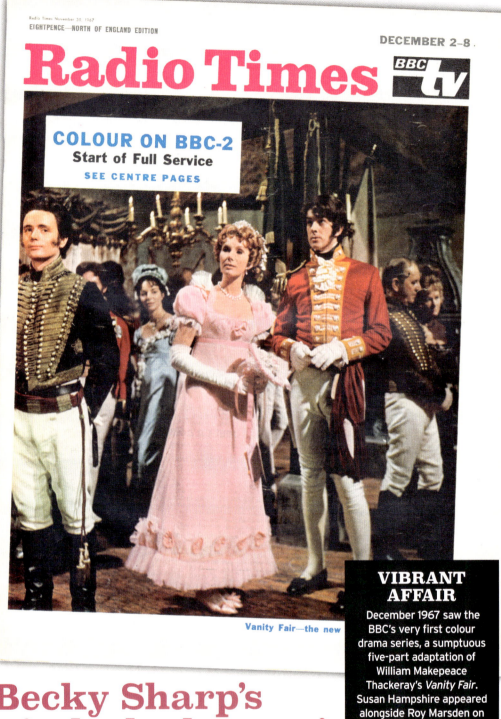

VIBRANT AFFAIR
December 1967 saw the BBC's very first colour drama series, a sumptuous five-part adaptation of William Makepeace Thackeray's *Vanity Fair*. Susan Hampshire appeared alongside Roy Marsden on the *Radio Times* cover

'Becky Sharp's wig looked green'

Susan Hampshire's star was in the ascendant in the 1960s. She won lead roles in a trio of major BBC period dramas – *The Forsyte Saga, Vanity Fair* and (in 1969) *The First Churchills* – and, when they were eventually shown in the USA, she bagged Emmy awards for all three.

"David Giles, one of the directors of *The Forsyte Saga*, chose me for Becky Sharp," she tells *RT* in 2022. "I'm very fond of Becky. Another nasty person [like Fleur Forsyte] but way ahead of her time with her energy and chutzpah. I adored working with David on *Vanity Fair*. He encouraged you to have a free rein. Actors are often critical of other actors, and even if they thought what you were doing was rubbish, David gave you freedom to explore your character. There was trust between us as director and actress."

Hampshire remembers it was a big deal making the BBC's very first colour serial. "Oh, there were huge adjustments for colour. As Becky, I had a red wig and at first it photographed green, so a lot of extra work went into getting that right. The skill of the hair and make-up artists and the costume department was absolutely phenomenal. Such talent and dedication."

If she found the rigmarole of making period drama sometimes painful, she's not complaining. "I am completely sanguine about the torture of wearing pins underneath the wig. It might be absolutely killing you, as well as the corsets and the shoes pinching, but I don't care – it's part of the story. And I was 100 per cent wanting to do what was right for the production."

BBC 2 COLOUR
WHERE IT ALL BEGINS

IN December, BBC-2's full colour service swings into action. Since July, viewers lucky enough to have colour sets have been able to see bright tartan kilts at the Beating of Retreat, and the delicate blues and greys of Persian temples.

But from December onwards the majority of BBC-2 programmes will be in colour—not only sport and documentaries, but variety shows and plays as well.

The coming of colour has meant changes in almost every department. At the Television Centre in west London, which is one of the largest centres of its kind in the world, producers, directors, technicians, props men, wardrobe and make-up staff, even writers, have been learning to 'think colour.'

Blazing the colour trail for drama will be a serial version in five parts of Thackeray's *Vanity Fair*, starring Susan Hampshire as Becky Sharp.

PERHAPS it is in costumes, particularly period ones like those in *Vanity Fair*, that the full glory of colour television will be seen. Since the earliest stages, Joan Ellacott, the costume designer and supervisor has been in on the planning of the serial. The costumes not only have to be correct in period, but have to tone with the set, the mood of the scene, the nature of the character, and the actor or actress's own colouring.

All the costumes have been specially designed for *Vanity Fair*, not taken from stock as they usually are, or hired. Joan Ellacott has spent hours with her sketch pad and pencil in the Victoria and Albert Museum, and the National Army Museum at Camberley, making drawings and notes.

From these sketches, patterns are made, and then the making begins, not only of dresses, but of accessories like handbags and hats. Here, the wardrobe have been working very closely with the make-up department, the wig side especially.

Experience has taught them that unless hats and wigs are fitted in close conjunction, they are both liable to come off together!

LOOK SHARP

In rare photos from the *RT* archive, Susan Hampshire (above) looks at dress designs for her character Becky Sharp with BBC costume designer Joan Ellacott (in brown), while make-up artist Toni Chapman (left) arranges Hampshire's wig

1968
BRINGING YOU THE OLYMPICS

MEXICO 68

'Covering the 1968 Olympic Games is our biggest-ever sports operation,' said Peter Dimmock, general manager of BBC-tv's Outside Broadcasts. 'But just at the moment, in view of what's happening in Mexico, we are keeping our fingers crossed and hoping that everything goes off all right.'

If the run up to the nineteenth Olympiad has been marked by bullets and boycotts, the preparations for the mammoth international TV operation have been sweetness and light.

Says Peter Dimmock: 'It's a team operation to which everyone contributes, and the success depends on everyone taking part.'

Four of the world's major television organisations have combined to bring you the Games. They are the European Broadcasting Union, N.H.K. (Japan), T.S.M. (Mexico), and A.B.C. (America). All have supplied staff and equipment for the pool operation.

FEELING THE HEAT

The lead-up to the Mexico Olympiad was marred by civil unrest and student protests – and the shooting of hundreds of civilians by the military. The Games still went ahead. *Radio Times* sent Don Smith to Mexico to photograph landmarks (right) and Barry Wilkinson was commissioned to illustrate the cover (opposite page). The British athlete depicted is surely David Hemery, who went on to win gold in the 400m hurdles

87

Radio Times
The Sixties 1968

RADIO TIMES *September 19, 1968*

Have you ever stood on sand so hot that you burned your feet? Or tried to find a Nomad encampment in the middle of a desert? Or seen a mirage? When we loaded up our Landrover here at the Television Centre we didn't know what was ahead of us—but all these things happened, and a lot more besides! We took these pictures on our first day in Morocco—so here's our first look at the Arab world.

Valerie Singleton
John Noakes
Peter Purves

Blue Peter's Safari to Morocco

First stop—a chance for our Landrover to cool down in the shade on the hill overlooking Moulay Idriss—the Holy City of Morocco

Even in his lightweight cotton clothes John was sweltering. Maybe in the head to toe covering of the traditional Moroccan 'djelaba' he'd have been a lot more comfortable

Once through the gateway of Rabat, Morocco's capital city, we were in the Medina with its teeming alleys and markets—home of some of the finest craftsmen in the world

RADIO TIMES September 19, 1968

Radio Times
The Sixties 1968

The world-famous Moroccan carpets are made here in Rabat—not by machine or even by gnarled old craftsmen, but by dozens of children, some of them only about nine years old

This is the Hassan tower, the biggest minaret in the whole of Morocco. Val and Peter are resting in the shade—so guess who climbed to the top!

Can you imagine doing this in Piccadilly Circus? When the temperature's up in the hundreds, you just don't care! But this was only Rabat—the really hot bit was ahead of us. Just after John took this snap we were in our Landrover heading south for the Sahara, where water's more precious than gold and you don't even waste it on cleaning your teeth! You can share our adventures on Monday and Thursday when Blue Peter returns this week

'I fell off a camel'

Opening young viewers' eyes to the world, *Blue Peter* began its foreign expeditions in 1965, starting with Norway. In 1966, it was Singapore and Borneo. "That was the most interesting because nobody was going into Borneo and we spent the day with Dayak head-hunters," **Valerie Singleton** tells *RT* in 2022.

She vividly recalls the team's 1968 sojourn in Morocco. "It was so hot and dusty, and they're not great pictures of me because I had short hair. One night we accidentally ran over a goat on a mountain road – I was absolutely horrified. When we were down in the desert, there was a sign saying, 'Timbuktu 3,000 miles', and we were filming with camels that had been in *Lawrence of Arabia*. They get up quickly, and nobody told me that once you get on a camel, they lurch forward and backwards, and I fell off and landed in the sand."

A deadlier encounter occurred at a remote hotel. "One night I was so hot I took my mattress out to sleep by the pool. I had my foot raised. Something must have just brushed me and I looked down and there was a big black scorpion with his tail raised. God was on my side then. I just brought my leg back and went, 'Urgh!' So those were some of the hazards."

89

Radio Times
The Sixties 1968

One in the eye for JOHNNY

Although the current series of *Animal Magic* is coming to an end, the summer will not be spent just playing with Dottie, the lemur. Johnny Morris and Keith Shackleton are using the next few months to find unusual and exciting subjects for a fresh autumn series.

Johnny will be putting on his seven-league boots and completing an itinerary which includes a visit to an African wildlife reserve with African school children, becoming involved with wildlife conservation in its practical sense, and animal collecting for zoos.

Johnny will also look at some of the animals at Basle Zoo, including a friendly Indian rhino, and a fine group of African elephants.

Keith Shackleton will visit the Camargue in the South of France with paint brushes and easels, to capture the animals of the area on canvas.

All this, and more, in *Animal Magic* in the autumn.

TALK TO THE ANIMALS
A staple of children's television for 21 years (1962–83), *Animal Magic* was hosted by Johnny Morris. Like a sweet-natured Dr Dolittle, he would talk to his animal friends and lend them comical voices of their own

RADIO TIMES July 11.

RADIO TIMES June 20, 1968

BASIL BRUSH

Lots of people write and ask me how I ever got mixed up in showbusiness. Well, it all started when my father got tired of being chased around the countryside and decided to retire to the City. For the peace of it, you know.

The family set up lair in Green Park, right by Buckingham Palace (because the neighbours are so nice there).

One day my friend Freddy got two seats for the Television Theatre and he asked me if I would go along. Of course, I was delighted because it was Mr. Nixon's show and he was up to his magic tricks.

He asked for a volunteer to help out, and in just two shakes of a fox's tail I had jumped onto the stage. And there I was on TV. Me!

One thing led to another and since then I've been doing rather well in showbusiness.

BOOM! BOOM!
Designed by Peter Firmin and voiced and operated by Ivan Owen, posh glove-puppet fox Basil Brush began life on ITV. He was given his own show on BBC1 in 1968, assisted by "Mr Rodney", ie *The Likely Lads'* Rodney Bewes

For your Scrapbook

The Magic Roundabout

Brian found

DYLAN

sitting under a tree

He was playing his guitar so loudly that Mr. McHenry hurried off to see what all the noise was about

Look out for Mr. McHenry next week

Hmm! Paint and brushes. I wonder if Zebedee would paint a picture for me, says

FLORENCE

of

The Magic Roundabout

Look out for Zebedee next week

MERRY-GO-ROUND
The Magic Roundabout was a hugely loved animation that ran for many years in the timeslot before the BBC1 evening news. Eric Thompson voiced each episode, making up new stories overlaid on the original French pictures

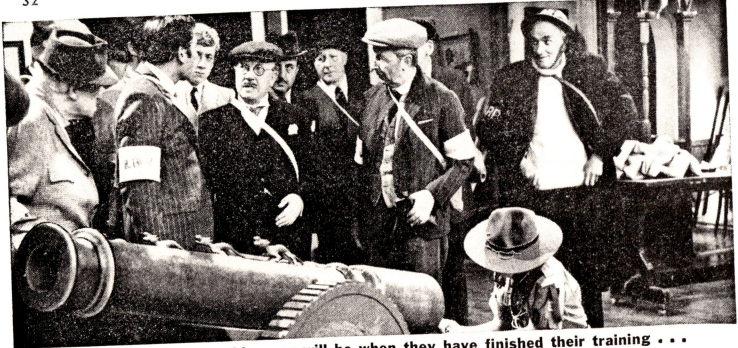

They are ready to face anything—or will be when they have finished their training...

DAD'S ARMY

Russell Twisk introduces a new comedy series about the men of Britain's Home Guard and some of their Finest Hours

1 Wed Do the initials L.D.V. mean anything to you? Do they start you on a journey down memory lane? If not, then you probably weren't around when that vintage Dunkirk spirit was in the air back in 1940—and Hitler was threatening to start an invasion.

The name Local Defence Volunteers soon gave way to the more popular Home Guards. These men formed themselves into small local units: wangled as many uniforms and weapons as they could and set about preparing themselves to fight to the finish.

Wednesday's new comedy series, *Dad's Army*, is about the formation and adventures of a small Home Guard unit at Walmington, somewhere on the south coast of Britain. The local bank manager Mr. Mainwaring decides to answer the call, and sets about recruiting.

The idea for the series came to Jimmy Perry—who was a sixteen-year-old member of the L.D.V.—while he was watching the Changing of the Guard outside Buckingham Palace. In wartime, he remembered, the Home Guard stood sentry, and as he walked back through St. James's Park he started to see the possibilities for a TV comedy.

Producer David Croft, who is also co-author, was called up to the army before he could join the L.D.V., but he has been careful to get the props and the flavour for the series just right. One difficulty was the scarceness of uniforms: 'Home Guard uniforms are almost as hard to get today as they were in wartime,' he says.

It is no accident that all the main characters are portrayed by actors who have a military background. Much care has been taken not to cheapen the efforts of the Home Guard. Although they never, in fact, had to face an invasion, or fire a shot in anger, they were all determined to fight to the bitter end to stop any German invasion.

Three fine comedy character actors—Arthur Lowe, John Le Mesurier, and Clive Dunn—play the leading parts. All three were in the army: though none was in the Home Guard.

Arthur Lowe plays Mainwaring, the bank manager who takes command. 'He is as keen as mustard: typifies the spirit of the times,' says Lowe.

His number two, Sergeant Wilson, is played by John Le Mesurier whose doleful features have peered out of countless films—in fact, during a weekend off from *Dad's Army* he nipped over to Venice for a day's filming with Fred Astaire. Le Mesurier served in India during the war, mainly on the North-West Frontier.

Clive Dunn plays Lance-Corporal Jack Jones, the butcher who can lavish a bit of best frying steak to get in with the officers. Clive joined the army a week before the L.D.V.s were formed (May 14, 1940) and he spent his first few months washing-up. Later he was sent abroad, captured in Greece, and made a P.O.W. above a hairdresser's shop in Austria. He did see the Austrian Home Guard in action though. 'Yokels with guns,' he calls them.

Dad's Army will bring memories flooding back for anyone who remembers the days of Dunkirk. It may even—as producer David Croft says—' make father's wartime reminiscing respectable.'

But although *Dad's Army* is set very firmly in wartime—the fun itself is timeless. Why not join the little community of Walmington on Wednesday as they face a probable invasion ... and decide to answer the call?

Pistol practice for keen-as-mustard Mainwaring, the bank manager who is in command of Walmington's Home Guard Unit and more than ready to have a go ...

Clive Dunn as Lance-Corporal Jack Jones, the local butcher now in charge of the cavalry division. Can it be that he is the right man for the job?

DON'T PANIC!
Dad's Army is such a familiar classic now, it needs no introduction but it did when it was brand new back in July 1968. The beloved sitcom would run for 80 episodes across nine series – and has been repeated umpteen times

ERIC & ERN
The comedy duo's first BBC show *Running Wild* had flopped in the 1950s, but they were on the up after a run on ITV and, once teamed with writer Eddie Braben back at the BBC, their glory days began. In 1968, they spoke to *RT* reporter Gay Search and posed for Don Smith on 29 June

They're Back!

Eric Morecambe and Ernie Wise return in a new BBC-tv series after thirteen years' absence. Here they chat about themselves and their life in show business

ERIC MORECAMBE is much shorter than he looks on the telly.

'I'm not really tall,' he said, and pointing at Ernie Wise he added, *It's just that he's a midget*.'

Morecambe and Wise are back with the BBC after an absence of thirteen years.

'I was looking at some old scripts the other day of a radio show we did shortly after our first television series thirteen years ago. It's a scene where someone says to Eric, "Are you Eric Morecambe?"'

'And I say, "Have you got a television set?" He says, "No," and I say, "Yes, I'm Eric Morecambe".'

'It went down as badly as that!' added Ernie.

They still remember it. 'You never forget something like that in spite of anything else that happens afterwards.'

'There's that old gag—someone says, "Your act is terrible," and you reply, "You're a hundred thousand pounds too late," or "Yeah, I'm crying all the way to the bank."

'But that's only a façade. No matter how successful you are, it still hurts if people don't like you.'

They've been together now for twenty-eight years—'*I'm thinking of divorcing him, he talks too much*'—very successfully without any quarrels. All their decisions are mutual.

'We split everything right down the middle, sixty per cent for me, and forty per cent for Eric.'

Ernie is the one who bears most of the responsibility for running the business side—'*He's a great little business manager. Great. A lousy actor and a lousy straight man, but a great little business manager!*'

For the past five or six years they've been riding the crest of the wave.

'It's our turn, that's all.'

'We've always said since the big time started for us that we'd got until we were fifty-five, and after that...'

'The hardest thing in comedy is to grow up. We can't still be doing in ten years' time what we're doing now.

'I mean, we can do a sketch with a pretty young girl now and that's fine. In ten years' time, if we did it we'd be looked on as lecherous old men.'

They both find that people expect to see them together in public.

'They tend to think of me as his keeper, and ask where is he, and is he all right. I am surprised they don't ring me up and say, "He didn't come in till two a.m. the other day".'

'Half-past eight in the evening more like. Hey, hey. I once bought some things from a shop in Liverpool, and when Ern went in there by chance a couple of hours later they told him everything I'd bought —"He had that sort of cheese, a jar of those pickles..."'

As they have both been in show business together since they were fourteen, the thought of being anything other than comedians always seems very strange. 'I might have gone into business, I suppose, and done a bit better than the next man...'

'*No you wouldn't, Ern, you'd have been a millionaire. I'd have been a thief. Raffles and all that, white gloves, and a little moustache.*'

'You *are* a thief—where do you think all those gags come from?'

Off stage they see little of each other. 'We're together all day long and anyway we live miles apart.' And they both welcome the peace and quiet of their respective homes. 'It gives you a sense of proportion. I mean, Clark Gable's wife didn't swoon when she saw him, like the woman in the two-and-nines.'

'When I get home after a show, the wife says, "You haven't cleared out that attic. The show was good, but you haven't cleared out that attic"!'

Something that's been puzzling thousands of people for a long time now is the joke with which Eric and Ernie finish their show. All we ever hear is the first line— 'There were these two old men sitting in deckchairs...'—and having heard how it ends from Eric, I think it's probably best that way.   GAY SEARCH

93

Radio Times
The Sixties 1968

RADIO TIMES March 21, 1968

BBC-2 COLOUR

LATE-NIGHT FIXTURE
RT caught up with Joan Bakewell in March 1968. She hosted BBC2's arts show Late Night Line-Up from 1965 to 1972, and in later years fronted BBC1's Heart of the Matter and Sky's Portrait Artist of the Year

Not only attractive... but also very intelligent

Joan Bakewell of Late Night Line-Up is interviewed about interviewing by Gay Search

'THE thinking man's fancy': that's what Joan Bakewell has been called in a typically condescending way by certain male Fleet Street journalists. Time and again, men make the amazing discovery that here is a woman who is not only extremely attractive, but also very intelligent. Many of them admire her for it, others in spite of it, but a few resent it strongly.

David Susskind, the American film and television producer, was one of the few, and during the interview Joan was trying to conduct he kept making statements of 'the woman's place is in the home' variety. At the time Joan was furious. Now she is more philosophical about it.

'If only I'd *known* he was going to start that old argument, I'd have loved it. But I was so unprepared.'

Surprisingly, the Susskind interview isn't the one she hated most of all. 'It's the very boring ones, those that sink without trace that are the worst.'

Fortunately not all Joan's male 'victims' react like Susskind. Frank Muir certainly didn't. 'Being interviewed by Joan induces a kind of schizophrenia. The mind doesn't know whether to concentrate on keeping one's side of an interview going—or looking at the delectable Mrs. B. I suppose you'd call it "the agony and the ecstasy"!'

When I spoke to Joan she was interviewing Martin Davies the new director of the National Gallery, and as paintings are one of her great passions she was busily gleaning for herself as much information as she could.

'I always enjoy interviewing someone who's passionately interested in his job, whatever it is. It's marvellous when the subject happens to be one I'm particularly interested in, and when it's one I know nothing about I usually come away thinking: "Gosh, I never knew that sewers, or whatever, could be so fascinating."'

In many of the interviews she does, her deep curiosity conveys itself to the viewer. She seems to 'catch fire' on some subjects, and can often be found still talking to her guest long after the programme is over.

Interviewing and its responsibilities have been in the news rather a lot recently—and the question has been raised of how far an interviewer can legitimately probe.

'There's nobody I wouldn't interview,' Joan said, 'but there are certain personal questions that I wouldn't ask. And anyway,' she added, 'the last way to get *that* sort of information is to ask for it!'

Joan is relieved that Late Night Line-Up doesn't require the really tough cross-examination type grilling of politicians that other programmes do. She has interviewed people like Sir Edward Boyle and Ernest Marples, but not about politics.

And it was only after Jo Grimond had relinquished the leadership of the Liberal Party that she interviewed him. 'I was able to ask him questions I could never have asked before —or at least could never have got answers to before!'

Her television appearances haven't really caused any problems for Joan. In fact the only member of the family who's affected by them is her eight-year-old daughter Harriet. At school she finds that lots of her classmates' remarks are prefaced with, 'Just because your Mother's on the telly ...'

But Harriet has a very sensible answer for that. 'It's just a job like any other,' she tells them.

Joan herself finds fame no problem. Few people recognise her in the street and those that do tend to think that they know her from somewhere else—not the box.

A short time ago, Joan had a new carpet fitted, and once the job was done, the workman asked her to fill in a form. As she was doing so he said: 'I know that face, don't I?'

Joan, feeling rather confused, told him he might. 'Well, even if I didn't know the face,' he replied, 'I'd know those legs anywhere.'

RADIO TIMES December 26, 1968

For Fanny Cradock, it all began in the blackout

FIERY FANNY
Fanny Cradock, flanked by husband Johnnie, had dished out culinary advice on the BBC since the 1950s. She was a formidable character. *RT's* Don Smith recalled, "Once when I asked to take her picture, she thrust her kitchen knife at me, shouting, 'Get away from me!'"

That's when she met Johnnie—'and he pointed me in the right direction'

TURN left past the Watford roundabout, drive down a narrow lane, then follow your nose to the elegant house dating back to 1715 which stands in three acres belonging to Fanny and Johnnie Cradock.

That is as vague as they asked me to be about their whereabouts because over-eager souvenir hunters used to carry off parts of their former home in South London. They don't want it to happen again.

The Cradocks have just moved into the house and are having it drastically altered while they live in the only habitable rooms—the bedrooms.

We sat in the hall amid the builders' rubble, surrounded by unplastered walls, with cardboard covering the parquet on the floor. Next door the workmen hammered away, while Fanny had Johnnie pour us all drinks.

First things first, said Mrs. Cradock. Fanny and Johnnie are partners—she wished to stress that straight away. 'I know about the food—he knows about the wine.

'When we met on Hackney Marshes in the blackout in 1939 he took me by the scruff of the neck and said: "Right." He stopped me galloping away in all directions at

by Russell Twisk

once. If it hadn't been for Johnnie I'd have been a flibbertygibbet. You must make that point.'

Johnnie the ex-Harrovian sat by, smiling, sipping his drink, the monocle firmly screwed in place.

Mrs. Cradock is a cooking and conversational happening. She has an ear for the outrageous, aware that she is eminently quotable. Alone she has brought those missing ingredients to TV cooking—flamboyance and showmanship.

Her *Colourful Cookery* series on BBC-2 has been a plum pudding stuffed full of memorable ad-libs, a rich assortment of bizarre tips. She shocked some of the audience by using paint and distemper brushes to make Palmiers. Her regular programme now is *Adventurous Cooking* on BBC-1 on Sunday afternoons.

None of her shows is scripted: 'I started talking on TV in 1953, and I've never stopped since.'

The first TV show had them both 'cross-legged with apprehension.' In fact Johnnie had to be literally kicked on to the stage.

Mrs. Cradock talks in a breathless, deep voice, once described as a 'circular saw going through a gin-soaked sheet.' She says: 'I'm always being called "Sir" on the telephone.'

Her voice is a gift to comedians, comediennes, and amateur imitators. She doesn't mind a bit. Her assistant once told a friend who asked if 'poor Mrs. Cradock was going to sue': 'Mrs. Cradock is trying to work out a way to pay Betty Marsden.' (Betty is Fanny Haddock of *Round the Horne* fame.)

The Lady Macbeth of Cooking, Lady Chef, the High Priestess of the Kitchen, Queen of British Cooking—they are just four of the tags given Mrs. Cradock by journalists. Only the last really annoys her: 'I don't cook British at all—get that

> **'I've never met a woman who was a good cook who is divorced, unmarried, or even widowed'**

right. I was brought up in France, all my cooking is based there, I have never learned anything from a British cook which I didn't know already.'

The British, she feels, are preoccupied with hygiene: 'They are far more interested in the facilities for flushing the "toilet" (put that in quotes and then they'll know I'm laughing). Whereas we will happily go down the garden to the privy as long as Madam is cooking a superb meal.

'But the greatest handicap of all facing the British housewife who wants to cook is the British husband—who just wants what Mum used to make.'

The Cradocks have been married for almost thirty years, and have spent only four days apart. Says Fanny: 'I've never met a woman

> **'I've never learned anything from a British cook that I didn't know already'**

who was a good cook who is divorced, unmarried, or even widowed.'

Then, more seriously, she added: 'Johnnie is Taurus, the bull, I am Pisces, the creative wild one. Your readers who follow the stars will understand why we get on.'

They both share an interest in mysticism, which they decline to talk about in public.

Both have French blood in their veins, they were both weaned on the good life, but the family fortunes didn't survive the second world war. As Mrs. Cradock explains: 'Cooking was the only way in which we could live as we love living.'

They both intend to keep living the good life. Johnnie is already planning large parties for the new house: 'You could lose 300 people here,' he said. And Mrs. Cradock says they'll never retire, but perhaps 'ease up eventually.'

It is still a rule in the Cradock household that no week passes without their creating something new in the kitchen. A rule they intend to keep.

> **'The British housewife's greatest handicap is the British husband'**

95

RADIO TIMES May 30, 1968

RADIO TIMES MAGAZINE

TOP OF POPS

CHART TOPPER

Top of the Pops was in its fifth year in May 1968 when *RT* looked behind the scenes. The UK number one at the time was *Young Girl* by Gary Puckett and the Union Gap

Every Thursday —the latest on the pop scene

1 'YES, it's number one, it's top of the pops!' With that familiar cry TV's weekly pop show swings on to the screen. Each week Studio G at the BBC's West London TV Centre is full of noise, colour, and action from the groups and singers—and the teenagers who dance their way through the show.

RADIO TIMES May 30, 1968

THE POPS

Top of the Pops, apart from keeping you up to date on the pop scene, also gives a fairly accurate guide to what's the latest in fashion—maxi skirts were pretty much in evidence from the show's early days.

This dancing audience—their ages range from fifteen to nineteen—are selected by John Hughes, the production assistant who makes regular tours of the clubs to find the really good dancers.

Some of them appear quite often—in fact, one boy actually started getting fan mail.

'The regulars get used to the cameras moving around the studio,' says Colin Charman, the producer, 'and that makes our job a whole lot easier.'

The morning after—Friday—planning for the next week's show begins. The production team listen to all the new releases—'every single one of them ' says Colin Charman with a suffering expression on his face. Then they decide on the two tips-for-the-top that are featured every week. American records, particularly when the artists aren't in this country, present quite a problem, so Top of the Pops have to make special films and these are done over the weekend.

On Monday, the Top of the Pops crystal ball comes out and they try to guess what will be where in the pop papers' charts the following day, and start planning the programme accordingly.

They write scripts, decide on the set and the lighting, and plan what to do with their newest piece of equipment, the audio-visual lighting effects machine.

On Tuesday they finally get the charts from the pop papers and confirm the contents of the programme.

For the next two days there is one hectic rush with rehearsals going on until shortly before 7.30 on Thursday, when that well-known voice cries yet again: 'It's number one, it's top of the pops!'

GAY SEARCH

Radio Times
The Sixties 1968

RADIO 1 CLUB

'Stevie Wonder just turned up'

After a triumphant first year of life, in October 1968 Radio 1 launched its new weekly show, the Radio 1 Club, prompting Radio Times to begin its own regular round-up of "the whole pop scene". The DJs had become bona fide celebrities themselves – with **Tony Blackburn** even releasing singles as a pop singer. He was ubiquitous on BBC1 on Crackerjack, Juke Box Jury and Simon Dee's chat show Dee Time, and fronting Time for Blackburn! on ITV.

"When I went on the air with the breakfast show on Radio 1 every morning, there were around 21 million people listening," he tells RT in 2022. "So practically overnight you could make a name for yourself. And with Top of the Pops as well [he joined in spring 1969], it was massive. You couldn't do that now because there are so many radio and TV stations, but back then it was so powerful."

Blackburn had idols of his own – and managed to meet most of them. "Yes, I toured with Diana Ross and the Supremes. Met the Four Tops many times. I got very friendly with Richard and Karen Carpenter. And Gene Pitney, funnily enough. I used to go to breakfast with him in the 60s when he was in London. He had a big audience in this country, more so than in America actually. So he used to tour here a lot and sometimes if he was in London, he'd ring me up and say, 'Fancy coming out for breakfast?' and we'd go out for a chat. A lovely guy. The only person I didn't meet was Marvin Gaye. I'd like to have met him.

"I got to know Stevie Wonder through Top of the Pops. I went into his dressing room and he was sitting there playing the piano. We became really friendly."

Many years later, Blackburn was hosting Soul Night Out on BBC Radio London. "The very first one was at the National Club in Kilburn. It held 2,000 people and on the first night they didn't think anybody would show up, but over 5,000 came. Even I found it difficult to get in! Halfway through the live programme one of the guys said to me, 'Stevie Wonder has turned up.' We hadn't booked him. He'd just popped up to thank me for playing Motown and came on the stage and sang one of his songs."

97

Radio Times
The Sixties 1968

RADIO TIMES *September 26, 1968*

The Sandie Shaw Supplement

'I DON'T mean to be pompous,' said Sandie Shaw biting her lower lip. Sitting in her agent's plush office, high above the roar of London's Regent Street, dressed like a Red Indian. 'Meet the Queen of the Wigwam,' said Eve Taylor, the agent.

Sandie's brown face was half-obscured by a hanging fawn headband, her eyes peered out through her maxi sunglasses. It would be impossible for her to *look* pompous. But then she was talking thoughtfully about her career, and she takes that seriously.

'I'm not going to keep going in this business until my mind goes stale, until I do things I've done before because I know it works. That's what they call an "all-round entertainer", and I don't want to be one of those. If anyone calls me a new Vera, Gracie, or anything, I'll scream.'

Sandie Shaw, twenty-one, newly married, affluent, the world at her bare feet. Her new series on BBC-1 has started. She hopes that people are thinking 'more kindly of me' after seeing it. Eve Taylor thinks it will 'surprise people.'

When Sandie says how determined she is not to get stuck in her career—'I'd go back to being plain Sandra Goodrich rather than keep doing the same old things'—she adds: 'I didn't leave one dead end for another.'

This spectre of Sandra Goodrich (Sandie changed her name when she made her first disc) and the giant motor works at Dagenham, where she was a punch-card girl, never seem far away when Sandie is talking about herself.

But Dagenham also has a special significance of another kind. She nurses its image as a zealous M.P. might relate his success in politics to his constituency.

She feels that if the girls at Dagenham think that her TV series is a success, then it *is* a success. 'When we planned the shows, I thought about the girls coming home from work and watching telly, and what they would like to see. I know what I would have liked to have seen when I was one of them.'

Not that she is sentimental about the little 'ole village of Dagenham, and the old days. Because she loves being a star, being able to buy all the clothes she wants, being recognised. 'If I woke up tomorrow and found that this life was all a dream and I was back at the factory, I know that I would still get out.

'I said to myself at sixteen, "this isn't for you, Sandra." It never could be.'

Since her marriage in May to designer Jeff Banks, Sandie says, she is working even harder. 'He

98

RADIO TIMES *September 26, 1968*

Sandie... summer... and the sea

These pictures capture the mood of five sun-filled days spent this summer on the almost deserted beach at Pendine, Carmarthen. Sandie Shaw and a BBC-tv film unit were trying to capture the atmosphere of various subjects for

The Sandie Shaw Supplement

is very busy working most of the time, so there's nothing for me to do but work.'

Husband Jeff helps her: 'If I do something well, he spoils me, something not well, and he nags.' She laughed after she'd said that.

What will she do after the BBC series? Sandie looked at Eve, and Eve obliged. Like an airline announcer, she reeled off a list of places round the world—'Australia, Africa, Italy, Sweden, the States...'

Ever since Sandie made her first record — which flopped — people have been saying that her success was only a flash in the pan. Some flash!   RUSSELL TWISK

IT'S SANDIE

Having become the UK's first ever Eurovision winner the previous year, Sandie Shaw turned 21 in 1968 and secured her own BBC1 show, *The Sandie Shaw Supplement*. Producer Mel Cornish told *RT*, "The title is intended to suggest the glossy world of the colour magazines" – a style echoed in this *Radio Times* spread

Radio Times July 10, 1969
London and South-East   July 12-18   EIGHTPENCE

Radio Times

Follow this week's historic adventure on BBC-tv and Radio

1969

BBC 1

6.0 a.m.-10.30
APOLLO 11
The First Man on the Moon

Shortly after 7.0 this morning astronaut Neil Armstrong should set foot on the moon. As he goes down the steps Armstrong will switch on the black and white television camera to beam live pictures back to earth. That transmission should also cover the moment when Edwin Aldrin joins Armstrong on the surface and continue throughout the two hours and forty mins. of the Moon Walk.

Before that more live pictures are expected from the Command Module as Michael Collins looks towards the moon and the landing ground from sixty miles up.

A report by **James Burke** with **Patrick Moore** from the Apollo Space Studio and **Michael Charlton** at Houston Mission Control
See page 26

★

1.0
APOLLO 11
Man on the Moon
Also on BBC-2 in colour

First footsteps on the moon. Soon after 7.0 a.m. Neil Armstrong and Col. Edwin E. Aldrin will leave the Lunar Module and walk on the moon's surface. BBC-1 will bring you live pictures of the moment the entire world has waited for

'It was extraordinarily intense'

In the summer of 1969, the build-up to the first Moon landing was intense, with constant updates from Patrick Moore and James Burke in the BBC's Apollo Space Studio. On the evening of 20 July, they stood by, ready to receive whatever Nasa broadcast via a single Atlantic satellite.

As Burke explained in RT 50 years later in 2019, "By now late evening in the UK, the astronauts' plan (and ours) was a night's sleep and then the moonwalk. But I heard them doing stuff to indicate a change of plan (preparing their moonwalk suits and not rigging sleep hammocks), so it was a time for a rethink – and the first ever BBC all-night TV.

'One small step' happened for a UK audience of 22 million at 3.56am."

In 2022, **James Burke** looks back again on that momentous night: "On camera, the first thing you learn about doing live TV is: 'Keep talking whatever happens.' And the second is: 'Explain what the viewer is looking at.' That night – Moon landing, first ever, unique world event – all I could think of was how to avoid going down in the annals as the guy who talked over the top of Neil Armstrong when he got to the bottom of the ladder. And then couldn't describe what we were looking at, out there across the lunar surface, because nobody had ever seen it before.

"Other than that, Mrs Lincoln...? It was the second most exhilarating experience of my life." He won't be drawn on the first. "Extraordinarily intense because in the brief periods between the end of an astronaut's last sentence and the beginning of his next, you had to do the explaining bit. In the unknown number of seconds available.

"I recall an Apollo astronaut once saying to me: 'There's so much to do. A mission's just so many minutes and seconds, all the way. No spare time to marvel.' I sometimes look back with disconsolate regret that I was too busy to marvel."

Radio Times
The Sixties 1969

RADIO TIMES *July 10 1969*

This week three men set out

Three men and their journey into space are about to rivet the attention of the world. Here JAMES BURKE introduces eight days of drama and suspense

THE MEN

COMMANDER

Neil A. Armstrong. *Born Wapakoneta, Ohio, August 5, 1930. Blond hair; blue eyes; 5ft. 11ins.; 11 stone 11lbs. B.Sc. in Aeronautical Engineering. Wife: Janet. Two sons: Eric—12, Mark—6.*

Neil Armstrong is a pleasant, ordinary-looking American. You'd pass him in the street and not look twice. But his conversation reveals a dry, prosaic character. He tends to talk very briefly and very much to the point. And the only thing he wants to talk about is space. He's very meticulous. In training the technicians who work with him say guardedly ' he's mission oriented.' What they mean is that he is not the outward-going casual man you warm to. But then as Commander of Apollo 11 he can afford even less than other Apollo Commanders to make a slip.

NASA say he's more Air Force than the Air Force, even though he's a civilian—he's described by almost everyone in NASA as ' probably the best jet test pilot in the world.' He distinguished himself as a fighter pilot in Korea.

He was selected as an astronaut in September 1962, and has since flown only once: as Commander of Gemini 8, launched March 16, 1966.

His home town has named a street after him. His school teachers remember him as ' single-minded and industrious.' He got his flying licence before he was old enough to drive a car. He read aeroplane magazines, not comics.

LUNAR MODULE PILOT

Edwin Aldrin *(Colonel, U.S.A.F.). Born Montclair, New Jersey, January 20, 1930. Blond hair; blue eyes; 5ft. 10ins.; 11 stone 11 lbs. B.Sc., Doctor of Science in Astronautics (Massachusetts Institute of Technology). Wife: Joan. Three children: Michael—13, Janice—11, Andrew—11.*

' Buzz ' is a bull of a man. The people who train him complain that *he* drives *them* too hard and apparently never tires. They also say he is the most pernickety astronaut there is. If something is wrong he wants to know every detail, however small.

' Buzz ' Aldrin is outwardly much the same as his Commander. He uses few words and is apparently almost without humour. He is reported never to make mistakes, and to be an enormously competent pilot. His care for detail should stand him in good stead. His job in the Lunar Module will be basically to monitor everything Armstrong does and check all systems throughout the flight down to the moon and back.

He was selected as an astronaut in October 1963 and has since flown once: as second pilot on Gemini 12, launched November 11, 1966. In fact he set a record for time outside the spacecraft—five-and-a-half hours. Aldrin has been called ' the astronaut's astronaut.'

COMMAND MODULE PILOT

Michael Collins *(Colonel, U.S.A.F.). Born Rome, Italy, October 31, 1930. Brown hair; blue eyes; 5ft. 11ins.; 11 stone 11 lbs. B.Sc. Wife: Patricia. Three children: Kathleen—10, Ann—7, Michael—6.*

Michael Collins is totally unlike his fellow astronauts on Apollo 11. He's of Irish descent and he spends a great deal of his time smiling and joking.

His job is mainly to fly the mother spacecraft in orbit while Armstrong and Aldrin go down to the moon and back. He shrugs this off philosophically—' somebody has to stay behind.'

If anything other than a serious ' getting on with the job while we make history ' feeling comes across on the live television broadcasts from this mission, it will be due in all probability to Collins. He was selected as an astronaut in October 1963. He has flown once, as second pilot on Gemini 10.

THE MOONCRAFT

THE ship in which the astronauts spend most of the journey and which serves as a base from which the Lunar Module operates on the trip down to the moon and back is called the Command and Service Module—CSM for short. It's made in two separable bits: the Service Module—a cylindrical section housing all the power units and the main spacecraft engine; and the Command Module—the spaceship's cockpit, and the only part of the vehicle that returns, in one part at any rate, to earth.

Inside the Command Module the crew lie on couches—built to fit them individually—alongside each other, and facing the pointed end of the ship. In front of them, from head to waist level, and from wall to wall, the instrument panel.

The Commander, on the left seat, has the flight control instruments. The Command Module Pilot, in the centre, sees to the fuel states and does the navigation. And the Lunar Module Pilot, on the right seat, monitors the systems that provide oxygen, power, and temperature regulations in the cabin. All three have hand-operated throttles on the arm rests of their couches—one for direction, one for power.

Beyond the foot of the centre couch, a well intrudes into the tip of the spacecraft. This houses the navigation instruments. The tip itself comes off and back into the cabin, to clear a hole through which the crew go to the Lunar Module.

There's about as much room inside the Command Module as there is in the front seat of a large family car. On the six CM flights so far, of the one-and-a-half million functioning parts on board, only three have ever gone wrong.

The Lunar Module is the world's first pure spacecraft. Never intended for flight in air, it is built with no regard to smooth aerodynamic shape. The four men who have flown in it so far (McDivitt and Schweickart on Apollo 9, Stafford and Cernan on Apollo 10) describe it variously: ' A tin foil joke '; ' It's like flying in a bath tub with somebody banging on the outside '; ' You look at it—and you think, they must be joking.'

Its awkward-looking shape is purely functional: a lower stage carrying four legs, an engine and fuel tank; an upper stage carrying controls, food, oxygen, fuel, an engine, and the crew.

The lower stage—31 feet leg pad to leg pad and nearly 11 feet high —carries the descent engine on whose power the crew lower themselves to the moon. It also acts as a launch pad for take-off. It's then left behind on the moon.

As on the Command Module— there are two computers: one to do everything, the other to check it.

The crew compartment in the upper stage is just big enough for two men in spacesuits. They stand at the controls. There's no room to sit, and, anyway, nothing to sit on. They sleep on the floor. Two triangular windows at eye level are the only view out.

None of the LM returns. The lower stage is left on the moon. The upper stage is fired into solar orbit before they come home. But it carries the most vital piece of hardware in the mission: the ascent engine. If that fails, Armstrong and Aldrin don't come home.

THE MISSION

JUST before one in the afternoon of Sunday, July 20, Armstrong and Aldrin leave Collins alone in the mother ship and drift through the tunnel to the Lunar Module. Twelve orbits around the moon and then they separate the two ships.

One orbit of inspection to see that everything looks right on the LM—and then the dive towards the landing site in a long curve that takes them almost halfway round the moon and ends 50,000 feet above the surface. The descent engine fires to begin the ' powered descent '—and, like a helicopter, the LM sinks towards the surface, slowing gradually until at a point 110 feet up they hover and inspect the landing area. They have only two minutes hover power in that descent engine to change their minds about where to land.

They go on down to five feet— the probes extending from the LM foot pads make contact with the surface, the engine automatically cuts out, and they fall the rest of the way.

Touchdown is planned for nine-twenty-two on Sunday evening.

The first few seconds after touchdown are critical—if the landing feels the slightest bit uncertain the crew flick the ' abort ' button and relaunch immediately. If all feels right, they take two hours to check out all the systems necessary for take off at the end of their period on the surface, and then swallow a sleeping pill. Four hours later they wake, eat, and at just after seven-twelve a.m. on Monday, July 21, Neil Armstrong goes down the ladder . . .

As he reaches the second rung down the ladder he pulls on a ring that sets a television camera working, and pictures of his first contact with the moon will be relayed to earth as it happens. Twenty-seven minutes later Aldrin follows him. They both spend a total of two hours and forty minutes on the surface, televised throughout.

Then, with the camera on the surface watching them, they return to the Lunar Module, sleep briefly, and at about seven on Monday night lift off to rejoin the mother spacecraft that Collins has been flying in orbit all this time. Back in the Command Module they jettison the Lunar Module and head for home. They return to no tumultuous crowds, no hand-shakes, no speeches. After the greatest journey in the history of man, Armstrong, Aldrin, and Collins will go into quarantine for twenty-one days. They will have left the American flag on the moon—but nobody knows what they will bring back. And nobody is taking any chances. History or no history.

RADIO TIMES *July 10, 1969*

for a day on the moon

MAN ON THE MOON 1

The astronauts: Neil Armstrong, Michael Collins and Edwin Aldrin. Armstrong, the mission commander, and Aldrin, the lunar module pilot, will drop to the moon's surface. Armstrong will be the first man to step on to the moon. Command module pilot Collins will stay in lunar orbit. If one of the team goes sick —then all three astronauts will be replaced by another trio. NASA officials claim they could replace six teams—if they had to.

Inside the command module

below Inside the lunar module

(*NASA artist's impression*)

Moment of separation . . . the lunar module breaks free from the command and service modules and makes for the moon

MAN ON A MISSION

In July 1969, *Tomorrow's World* stalwart James Burke, who was co-hosting the BBC's Apollo 11 coverage, prepared *RT* readers for the days ahead

Radio Times
The Sixties 1969

RADIO TIMES *July 10, 1969*

Everyone can

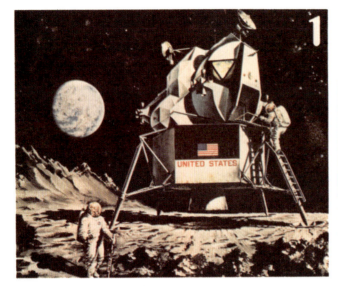

The strange world that awaits the astronauts—as seen by NASA's artists. 1. Safely on the moon. 2. Venturing away from the craft to obtain samples and place instruments. 3. Blast off! And back to the command module

The voices and pictures of the astronauts as they carry out their critical manoeuvres in space are fed back to Mission Control (6) in Houston, Texas, from Ground Stations around the world

From Armstrong's camera the television signal will go to the lunar module for transmission to earth. Any problems can be countered by erecting the S-Band antenna, illustrated above

RADIO TIMES July 10, 1969

go to the moon...here's how

The moment the world has waited for. This is Commander Armstrong, dressed exactly as he will be when he becomes the first man on the moon. Strapped to his chest: the camera which takes you with him

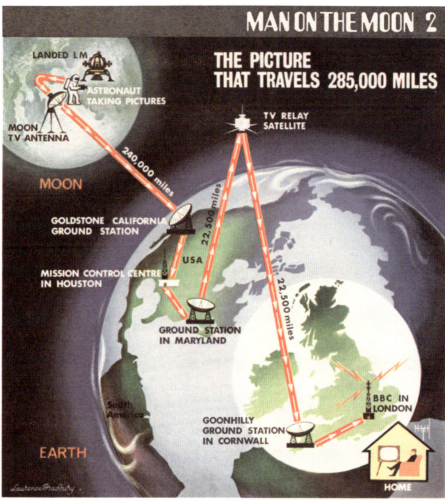

Helping to put you at home (9) completely in the picture are BBC-tv's special Apollo 11 space team—including Cliff Michelmore (7), Patrick Moore and James Burke (8). As well as interpreting the live pictures of this week's historic flight, they will be using models and film to fill in the complicated background. Full details of the coverage on BBC-1, BBC-2 Colour—and on Radio—are to be found on our programme pages

MOON WATCH

As anticipation mounted, *Radio Times* explained how the remarkable events would unfold and how the images would be beamed across space then relayed around the world and onto British TV screens

Radio Times
The Sixties 1969

RADIO TIMES July 31, 1969

TOMORROW IS HERE TODAY

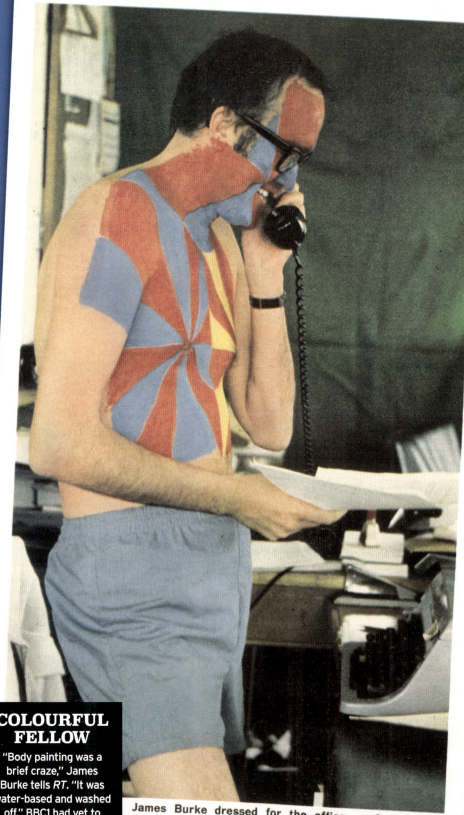

COLOURFUL FELLOW
"Body painting was a brief craze," James Burke tells *RT*. "It was water-based and washed off." BBC1 had yet to go into colour, so only *RT* readers would enjoy the full effect of this *Tomorrow's World* item

James Burke dressed for the office . . . A new body paint, a new item for the show, James is happy to oblige

The future is our business says RAYMOND BAXTER

of Tomorrow's World which is back on your screen this week

1 FAMILIARITY with the perils which confront the future of mankind may not always be everyone's cup of tea. But, happily, we at *Tomorrow's World* find that most people are not put off by the chance to glimpse the future—although they may not always like what they see.

Our brief is to report tangible achievements on the whole broad horizon of scientific and technological development and discoveries. So our camera teams rarely travel to see the horrors of Biafra to bring home the effects of malnutrition on the very young. What we do is show you the latest techniques to combat hunger—for instance, the way intensive undersea farming might one day ensure a richer harvest from the oceans of the world.

We do not gawp at the misery of the primitive peasant farmer and speculate on his future. Instead we say: 'Here is a plough developed especially for his use, which he can make for himself, using mainly his local materials.'

We try to keep abreast of events and intentions—especially in space exploration. We were thrilled to be the first television programme in Europe to be able to show the extraordinary measures taken by the Americans to prevent inter-planetary infection that might result from samples of the moon arriving back here on earth.

We say: 'Here is a system which will enable air-liners to land safely in all weather.' We try not to enter into the controversy of where they should or should not be allowed to land. But we will report and comment on the latest possibilities in off-shore airfield construction and high speed communication to city centres.

We are concerned with fact and possibility—rather than fear and prejudice.

And, lest we fall into the television hazard of taking ourselves too seriously, we will go quite a long way for a laugh.

Incredibly, in the past fifteen years science and technology have advanced farther and faster than in the preceding 150 years. Yet, curiously enough, there are still some who sneer at technology and those who have wrought these miracles. Fortunately for us all, this blinkered fringe—though vociferous and all-too-often encountered in high places—would appear to be a minority.

Meanwhile, we of the *Tomorrow's World* team are proud to number amongst our regular viewers people who admit to no particular interest in science, yet who watch because they like the way we do things. And most particularly, we are proud of our viewers from the ranks of the young of all ages.

One of my favourites was the grubby eight-year-old encountered recently in a sweet shop at the foot of the GPO Tower. After a prolonged and silent study he said: ''Ere mister, you're the *Termorrer's World* bloke aint cher?' 'No, chum,' I said, 'You are.'

106

STARDATE: 1969

Star Trek began its long voyage on BBC1 on Saturday 12 July, in what had previously been the *Doctor Who* slot. Though made in colour, the first 17 episodes were aired in black-and-white as BBC1 didn't go into colour until November. The first episode (see the listing, right) didn't feature key cast such as Nichelle Nichols and DeForrest Kelley (pictured below, with Leonard Nimoy and William Shatner)

RADIO TIMES July 31, 1969

5.15 STAR TREK

Today the moon—tomorrow the cosmos? The first is fact, the second is so far fiction. Nevertheless this new adventure series looks forward to a not-too-distant future when man will be exploring and colonising the worlds beyond us. The star-ship *Enterprise*, under captain James Kirk, is engaged in patrolling the new-found galactic oceans; and in tonight's first story, *Where No Man Has Gone Before*, it is ordered beyond the limits of explored space. It picks up the flight-recorder of a long-lost spaceship—which warns of a terrifying hazard ahead. Soon *Enterprise* faces disaster, while the captain faces a grim choice between friendship and duty.

Captain James Kirk...WILLIAM SHATNER
Mr. Spock................LEONARD NIMOY
Lt.-Cmdr. Gary Mitchell.GARY LOCKWOOD
Dr. Elizabeth Dehner.SALLY KELLERMAN
Dr. Piper.....................PAUL FIX
Engineer Officer Scott....JAMES DOOHAN
Alden......................LLOYD HAYNES
Sulu........................GEORGE TAKEI
Lt. Lee Kelso................PAUL CARR

See page 32

With USS Enterprise in the vast seas of space

Michael Williams fills you in on the background to the space age Captain Hornblower and his companions in adventure

1 It's a lonely, confined world, the United Space Ship Enterprise. One vessel voyaging through the cosmos, doggedly carrying out its job of protecting trade, overseeing colonies, putting down the odd brush-fire war. Performing a task which is, in fact, not very different from that which shabby British frigates did in the seven seas of earth about the end of the eighteenth century—though Enterprise, operating a hundred years from now, has far vaster seas to sail in, many more territories to police.

So it's no accident that the character of Captain James Kirk was defined by the originators of *Star Trek* as 'a space-age Captain Hornblower.' A man alone, self-doubting, self-driven. A wonderful part, but not easy.

William Shatner, the man who plays Captain Kirk, has the right professional equipment for the role. A Canadian, he was raised in the theatre in the strict disciplines of Shakesperian parts, so he knows all about how to get deep into a character. He's done Westerns, too, and the riding, roping, shooting that these entailed mean that he has the physical toughness for the job as well. He's a keen sportsman in private life as well as being a photographer and a dog-lover.

The officer in charge of all the marvellous scientific equipment aboard Enterprise is Mr. Spock. Half earthman, half 'alien'—his father was a native of the planet Vulcan—he has a brain almost as cool and calculating as the computer which is his special charge.

It's another intriguing characterisation for an actor to get his teeth into; and the actor involved is Leonard Nimoy. He was in the business at the age of eight, though at various times he has been thoroughly out of it as cab driver, cinema usher, pet shop assistant, and other kinds of odd-job-man. He's from Boston, and when off duty relaxes in the very earthly and not too scientific pursuit of 'do-it-yourself' home improvement.

Very different in outlook from the rather chilly Mr. Spock is Dr. Leonard ('Bones') McCoy, senior ship's surgeon. A southern gentleman from Georgia with a cynical exterior, he is really a humanist who'll always back man against the machine. The doctor is otherwise De Forest Kelley, and he's a real-life Georgia cracker who never left his home state until he was seventeen. He has worked in many TV series, among them *Rawhide* and *Bonanza*, and he's a Sunday painter whenever he has a Sunday off.

Then there's Montgomery Scott. Every ship has to have a chief engineer and every good

Aboard the USS Enterprise

ship has a Scottish one. This born nuts-and-bolts man who's come up through the ranks and doesn't care who knows it is played by another Canadian, James Doohan.

In real life his background concerns twentieth century spacecraft rather than twenty-first century spacecraft—he was a flier with the Royal Canadian Air Force in World War Two.

However, Enterprise is a big ship, so many more members of her 430-strong crew will be appearing as the series unfolds. And it is not an all-male crew either—there are some very pretty girls aboard.

Radio Times
The Sixties 1969

RADIO TIMES *February 20, 1969*

CIVILISA

'Like a rock-climb, three steps up, two steps down—but in the end... an ascent'

Sir Kenneth Clark writes

2 COLOUR
SUN 8.15
Rpt. Fri 9.5

At the end of Bernard Shaw's *Heartbreak House* there is a Zeppelin raid, and a tremendously loud bang, far louder in the theatre than those made by the actual bombs dropped by Zeppelins. Mr. Shaw then makes his heroine say, in an ecstatic voice, 'I do hope they come again tomorrow night.'

This line couldn't have been written after the bombing of Coventry or Dresden, and the fact is that although Mr. Shaw thought that society needed a good shaking, it never crossed his mind, writing in 1919, that civilisation could be obliterated. We feel differently now for a number of reasons. For one thing, we know that all the human values that are lumped together under the word civilisation have been obliterated once in Western Europe.

Our programme begins in modern Paris, which has been for so long the symbol of civilisation; but in sixth-century Paris there was no security of any kind, no knowledge of the past, no conception of the future, a rule based on torture and death. Yet only a few generations earlier Roman justice, Roman administration and the gigantic monuments of Roman architecture must have seemed indestructible.

It has happened once; it could happen again. And this seems to me a good moment to ask what produced that almost incredible episode. What is it that destroys a civilisation? First of all, fear: fear of invasion, fear of famine, fear of some universal disaster that makes it not worth while setting up house or even planting trees.

And then exhaustion, the feeling that we have bitten off more than we can chew. This can co-exist with a high degree of material prosperity, in which case it takes the form of cynicism and boredom.

Civilisation is none the worse for a little accumulated wealth, enough to provide mobility and leisure. But, far more, it requires confidence, confidence in the society in which one lives, belief in its laws and its philosophy, confidence in the power of reason.

The aim of my thirteen programmes is to show the stages by which this confidence was restored. They are not so much concerned with civilisation in the abstract, as with a series of civilising episodes. Each one of these has extended in some way, or ways, our human faculties, and although the first impetus behind these episodes usually fades away, something is left.

The history of European civilisation has been like a rock-climb, three steps up, two steps down; but in the end there has been an ascent. The great thing is to keep on the move, and not to hang on motionless in a panic.

Because these programmes are on television I have drawn much of my evidence from visible sources. I have been, literally, looking for civilisation, and have been allowed by the BBC to visit, with brilliant directors and a responsive camera crew, all the great works of art and architecture that I describe.

I speak in about 130 different locations. There is plenty to delight the eye. Music also plays a large part in the series and, in some of the early periods, will be a revelation to many viewers, as it was to me.

Nevertheless, I want to make it clear that this series is *not* a history of the arts. It is a history of life-giving beliefs and ideas made visible and audible through the medium of art.

The programmes are officially described as 'a personal view.' Well, obviously no-one could treat such a vast subject with detachment, and it would be very boring if he tried to do so. But I am conscious of some serious omissions.

I have a personal dislike of Louis XIV and Versailles, although Voltaire thought them the climax of all civilisation. I have an immense admiration for Goethe, but I could not see a way of making visible his many contributions to the European spirit. In the end I suppose that these historical prejudices are less important than a general attitude of mind.

I hold a number of beliefs that have been repudiated by many of the liveliest intellects of our time. I believe that order is better than anarchy, creation better than destruction; I prefer gentleness to violence and forgiveness to vendetta. On the whole I think that learning is preferable to ignorance, and I am sure that human sympathy is better than ideology.

Above all, I believe in the god-given genius of certain individuals, and I value a society that makes their existence possible. The programmes are full of heroes—saints, philosophers, poets, artists, mathematicians—even a few men of action.

They are only a small sample of the great men that Western Europe has produced during the last thousand years; and a few of them have emerged from conditions at least as unsettled and alarming as our own: Shakespeare himself is an example.

This should give us confidence that, in spite of such deadening pressures as bureaucracy and mass salesmanship, Western Civilisation is still alive.

108

TION

'On the whole I think that learning is preferable to ignorance, and I am sure that human sympathy is better than ideology.'

MAN OF THE WORLD

In 2014, **Don Smith** (interviewed by Andrew Duncan) told of the time he photographed historian Sir Kenneth Clark in France for the filming of his 1969 series *Civilisation*. "We ended up in Paris on 13 May 1968, the day the student riots started. If you didn't run fast enough, you got clubbed by the police. I thought how ironic to be working on a programme called *Civilisation*. People asked if I took a picture in the streets, and I said, 'Not likely.' I didn't want to be beaten up.

"A photoshoot had been arranged of Clark standing with Notre Dame in the background. It was my big moment. I had a minute or so to do it. The tripod was set up and he posed. Just as I had the shot nicely framed, he took out a cigarette. He was a heavy smoker. But in those days there were rules for *RT* covers — you couldn't show people drinking, smoking or in bed. How could I tell him he mustn't smoke? If he became moody, I wouldn't have a picture. What the hell should I do? I asked him to lower his right hand, a little more please, just a little bit more, until the cigarette was practically hidden... and that picture was used."

109

Radio Times
The Sixties 1969

RADIO TIMES *July 24, 1969*

The girls behind THE LIVER BIRDS

Carla Lane (left) and Myra Taylor—'full of great ideas and learning very, very fast'

1 CARLA LANE and Myra Taylor—who created *The Liver Birds* (played in the series by Polly James and Pauline Collins)—are two Liverpool ladies. But any suggestion that the comedy is based on the writers' personal experiences of flat-sharing is—whatever you may have read in the newspapers—false.

Carla explains: 'The truth is that I was married when I was seventeen, and Myra when she was eighteen. We went straight from our parents to our husbands. After the stories about us being young girls who share a flat in real-life, one newspaper discovered the mistake and ran a photo-feature about "the mini-skirted mums," which didn't delight us either. You can't win!

'We'd rather not give our ages—but we're both beautiful. Well, actually I'm thirty-nine, got a son of twenty, and Myra's a little younger, about thirty-four.

'We met at the Liverpool Writers' Club. I've been a member for six years, Myra for five. She read a short story and I got the feeling that she was on the same wavelength. When you've got a friend—and let's face it this is rare in women—with whom you can write, it's great, makes everything easier.'

Both started out writing more-or-less serious articles for magazines, but it was Carla who first stumbled on the discovery that they had a commercial talent for humour. 'I wrote a piece entitled "Holidays Hilarious" for a popular weekly.

'They changed a few words, which made me furious. I went into an artistic tizzy wondering how they *dare* make such alterations, but I've learned not to be so sensitive now. Concentrating on humour I found I couldn't go wrong, sold lots of bits to women's journals, and to radio.'

So Carla and Myra decided to have a go at television comedy. 'We wrote a programme titled *Up, Down And All Around*. It was in a rather ambitious style, about the frustrations of man, and we were told it was Spike Milliganish.'

Michael Mills, BBC-tv's Head of Comedy, didn't think the script was viable but the dialogue convinced him that the two Liverpudlians had the right talent and he asked them to submit something else.

Their husbands were intrigued and, perhaps, rather impressed. However, they preferred to keep their minds on their own jobs rather than make constructive suggestions.

'Myra's runs a greengrocer's business, mine's a naval architect. Neither wants to know about the Liverpool Writers' Club. In fact, my husband thinks we're a load of nuts. He says he'd sooner go and sit in the middle of a level crossing than come to our meetings!'

Using their imaginations, Carla and Myra devised a comedy format around two fancy-free unmarried girls and eventually—with the aid of seasoned professional scriptwriter Lew Schwarz—*The Liver Birds* was hammered into shape and premiered in the recent *Comedy Playhouse* series.

'Before we got into this business we had no idea what goes into a half-hour programme. You can spend nine hours discussing a story line, then somebody will notice an implausibility, a plot development that doesn't work, and the whole idea is scrapped and we have to start again.

'Poor Lew—he has been marvellously patient and tactful with us. We must be dreadfully exasperating but, under the circumstances, we've got on very well.'

Over, for a last word, to Old Pro Lew. 'The show keeps me in a state of delightful nervous tension. The girls have great ideas and newcomers' enthusiasm. I just supply the discipline of the trade. Must say they're learning very, very fast indeed and I doubt if it'll be long before they take over entirely on their own.

'I'll miss the trips to Liverpool. I'm from Glasgow and the two towns have similar atmospheres. As a science-fiction addict I've had the curious sensation, when driving into Liverpool, that I'm the victim of a warping of the space-time continuum on the M6 and am really arriving in Glasgow.' DAVID GRIFFITHS

RARITIES

The original version of *The Liver Birds* starred Pauline Collins and Polly James. The BBC wiped its recordings of the episodes so these rare photographs – recently discovered in the *RT* archive – are an invaluable record of the sitcom's earliest days. Don Smith took them on 3 January 1969

Radio Times
The Sixties 1969

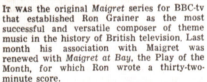

RADIO TIMES March 13, 1969

Ron Grainer
Mr Music of the small screen
talks with David Griffiths

WIZARD OF OZ
Throughout the 1960s, Australian-born composer Ron Grainer was the go-to man for catchy theme tunes: *Maigret, That Was the Week That Was, Steptoe and Son, Doctor Who, The Prisoner*... And in the 1970s, his TV earworms included *Tales of the Unexpected*

It was the original *Maigret* series for BBC-tv that established Ron Grainer as the most successful and versatile composer of theme music in the history of British television. Last month his association with *Maigret* was renewed with *Maigret at Bay*, the Play of the Month, for which Ron wrote a thirty-two-minute score.

Ron Grainer came to Britain in 1952 from his native Australia. He brought with him a saved-up £500, a wife, a step-daughter, and a competent piano technique—'But I couldn't get work as a pianist in London.'

After a while he gave up trying to make it as a musician and became part of a variety act, Allen Brothers and June. He says: 'We did a knockabout dance routine—very tough. Miss a trick and you got hurt. I was always nursing bruises.

'It was the era of the star American vocalists and we toured with them. If you saw Frankie Laine, Guy Mitchell, Billy Eckstine or Al Martino on the halls you also saw our act. In the afternoons I used to sneak into the theatres and play Mozart and Debussy on pit pianos in the dark.'

Between tours Grainer landed a job playing the piano for singers at a television company's auditions. This led to sporadic composing work for television plays.

'When cheques were late in coming we nearly starved,' he says. 'Our flat was free but my wife had to do cleaning in the block and I had to tend the boilers—getting up at five for three hours of stoking. Then another three at night.

'In between, I tried to write. But I kept meeting show-business people, and at last I started to earn good money as a pianist.

'Then the BBC asked me to write the music for the *Maigret* series. I had to choose between writing and playing. Now I only play on my own recording sessions.'

Which are plentiful.

Among the many other BBC programmes for which Ron Grainer has written the music are *Dr. Who* ('purely electronic'), *The Jazz Age* ('mixture of Chicago style jazz and Gershwin'), *Detective* ('unusual line-up of tamba—a Middle Eastern instrument—with violins, piccolos and celesta'), *Boy Meets Girl* ('medieval and Renaissance instruments including handbells, clavichord, light percussion and medieval fiddle with viola d'amore and oboe d'amore'), *Steptoe and Son*, *Comedy Playhouse*, *Oliver Twist* and *Old Curiosity Shop*.

There have been two stage shows—the hit *Robert and Elizabeth* and the flop *On the Level*—many short films, and a rapidly increasing number of features including *The Caretaker, A Kind of Loving, Nothing But The Best* and *Live Now, Pay Later.*

'Film and television writing suits me,' Ron says. 'I'm glad to be concerned with the visual arts. It's quite different from writing, say, your own symphony.

'You are writing to help what someone else is trying to achieve. You have to immerse yourself to a degree in somebody else's conception. You may express your own feelings but above all you must fit into a team.

'I regard the various musical instruments as like actors. You get a different kind of performance from each one. I'm always trying to find unusual combinations and instruments. My greatest, most impossible, dream is to own and play one of every instrument in the world.'

A milder Grainer dream has been realised. After seventeen years in Britain—the first eight of them poverty-stricken, the rest progressively prosperous—he now lives in Portugal.

'I like the climate, the food and wine are good, I love lying on a beach, and I intend to take life a little easier. I may also get more writing done. There's no phone—a great advantage because in London I've taken on too much work at times.'

112

RADIO TIMES 13 NOVEMBER 1969   BBC2   15 November Saturday tv   PAGE 29

BBC1

+++ APOLLO 12 +++
MISSION DAY TWO +++

10.0 am
Répondez S'il Vous Plaît
An invitation to learn French
with MAX BELLANCOURT
6: *Une carte pour l'Angleterre*
(shown last Sunday)

10.30
Wie bitte?
A beginners' course in German – 6
Introduced by LESLIE BANKS
(shown last Sunday)

11.0 Closedown

12.0 *Colour* ★
Weatherman
BERT FOORD
looks at the weekend weather

12.5
Casey Jones
The Lost Train: Searching for the lost Cannonball, Casey helps to capture a dangerous gang ‡

12.25
Charlie Chaplin
The Tramp
with
Edna Purviance, Ben Jamison
Charlie falls for the farmer's daughter and gallantly rescues her from a band of robbers. ‡

BBC1 in Colour ☆

Colour has come to BBC1. From today, the colour service will be available in the areas served by the transmitters at Crystal Palace (Ch 26); Sutton Coldfield (Ch 40); Winter Hill (Ch 55); and Emley Moor (Ch 44).
Crystal Palace operates in the area around London; Sutton Coldfield in the area around Birmingham; Winter Hill in South Lancashire; and Emley Moor in South Yorkshire.
For full information about the transmitters now in operation, and about those planned to come into operation in future, please turn to page 13. Consult your supplier for local information. Tuning information is given every night at 6.15 on BBC2. There is also a full programme of colour test transmissions on BBC2 – details page 49

12.45 *Colour*
Grandstand
Introduced by **Frank Bough**
BBC outside broadcast colour cameras bring you 4½ hours of top-class sport, featuring the Rugby League European Champions Cup; Racing from Cheltenham, including the day's top steeplechase, the Mackeson Gold Cup; International Gymnastics; and Motor Racing from Thruxton

12.55*
Football Preview
SAM LEITCH introduces *Grandstand*'s up-to-the-minute football preview, featuring the action and personalities in the news in today's League games and First Round FA Cup ties.

1.5, 2.10, 2.45*
Racing from Cheltenham
1.15 The Coventry Handicap Steeplechase (3 miles 1 furlong)
2.20 The Mackeson Gold Cup Handicap Steeplechase (about 2 miles and a half)
2.55 The November Handicap Steeplechase (2 miles)
Commentators PETER O'SULLEVAN and CLIVE GRAHAM
TV presentation by BARRIE EDGAR

1.25, 2.30, 4.45*
Motor Racing
The Grandstand Colour Trophy Meeting featuring the W. D. and H. O. Wills Formula 3 Trophy, and the Osram/G.E.C. Trophy Race for Saloon Cars.
Commentator at Thruxton
MURRAY WALKER
Special guest commentator
GRAHAM HILL
TV presentation by BRIAN JOHNSON

1.45*
International Gymnastics
The European International Trophy Meeting: a special invitation event at Fairfield Hall, Croydon, featuring the men's and women's individual champions from ten European countries.
Commentator ALAN WEEKS
TV presentation by ALAN MOUNCER

3.5*
The Rugby League European Champions Cup
for the Wills Trophy

BBC1 GOES COLOUR

Viewers staying up till midnight on Friday 14 November 1969 would have caught BBC1's very first colour programme, *An Evening with Petula* at the Royal Albert Hall. Saturday 15 November brought the first day of colour, as well as some black-and-white oldies (a Chaplin comedy from 1915!). An afternoon of colourful *Grandstand* led on to the first chance to see *Star Trek* in its many vibrant hues

BBC2

3.0 pm *Colour*
Saturday Cinema: The Baby and the Battleship
starring **John Mills**
Richard Attenborough
Puncher and Knocker, two British sailors ashore in Naples, are literally left 'holding the baby' – the baby brother of Knocker's girl friend. In desperation they smuggle the infant aboard their ship . . .

'Puncher' Roberts......JOHN MILLS
'Knocker' White
             RICHARD ATTENBOROUGH
Professor..............BRYAN FORBES
Captain............MICHAEL HORDERN
Marshal...............ANDRE MORELL
Maria..................LISA GASTONI
Screenplay by JAY LEWIS
and GILBERT HACKFORTH JONES
based on the novel by ANTHONY THORNE
Produced by ANTONY DARNBOROUGH
Directed by JAY LEWIS

4.30 Closedown

7.0 *Colour*
The News and Sport
and **Weather**

4.55*
Results Service
Times are subject to alteration in order to keep up to date. Latest football scores, racing results, and news are given throughout the afternoon, and the Teleprinter service is at 4.40*
Grandstand presented for television by
BRIAN VENNER
Edited by ALAN HART

5.15 *Colour*
Star Trek
This week: *Arena*
A treacherous attack obliterates the outpost on Planet Cestus Three and the USS *Enterprise* hurtles in hot pursuit of a mysterious alien vessel, only to be halted by an incredible occurrence.
The fantastic contest which follows is to try the strength and skill of Captain Kirk to the utmost, but it is not only these attributes which are on trial.

Captain Kirk....WILLIAM SHATNER
Mr Spock.........LEONARD NIMOY
Dr McCoy......DE FOREST KELLEY
Scott............JAMES DOOHAN
Sulu.............GEORGE TAKEI
Uhura..........NICHELLE NICHOLS
A Metron..........CAROLE SHELYNE

6.5 *Colour*
The News
Weatherman BERT FOORD

6.15 *Colour*
Simon Dee
introduces his guests
Musical director MAX HARRIS
Script JOE STEEPLES
Designer RAY PRICE
Director JAMES MOIR
Producer RICHARD DREWETT

† BBC recording
‡ Repeat
* Approximate time

7.15 *Colour*
Gardeners' World
with **Percy Thrower**
Fuchsias: 2 – Growing Fuchsias
Percy Thrower talks about the propagation and training of fuchsias for use as bushes, standards, or trailing plants.
Produced by BILL DUNCALF
Directed by JOHN CLARKE
(from BBC Midlands)

7.30
Rugby Special
Introduced by CLIFF MORGAN
The First English Trial
at the Reddings, Moseley
The first international against the Springboks is only a month away. It will present all the normal challenges to the selectors, but this year the England committee must be hoping that Don White, the newly appointed coach, will have gone a long way towards achieving the right blend of strength, skill, speed, and guile.
Directed by BILL TAYLOR
Series producer ALAN MOUNCER †

6.45 *Colour*
Dixon of Dock Green
starring **Jack Warner**
The Brimstone Man
by GERALD KELSEY
Dock Green Police find themselves in an unusual environment following an incident involving one of the students at a girls' teacher training college.

George Dixon.........JACK WARNER
Det-Sgt Crawford......PETER BYRNE
Det-Con Lauderdale
                     GEOFFREY ADAMS
Sgt Wills......NICHOLAS DONNELLY
PC Swain........ROBERT ARNOLD
WPC Reed..........JENNY LOGAN
PC York........HOWARD RAWLINSON
Harold Milton........NORMAN BIRD
Barbara............VICKI WOOLF
Jack Long........JEREMY YOUNG
Bill Harrison.......BILL TREACHER
Penny............PHILIPPA GAIL
Joan...............CAROL PASSMORE
Ann.............ROSEMARIE REEVES
Peter Clark........JOHN LONGMAN
Brian Parish.....LEROY LINGWOOD
Tate................TED CARSON
Robert Milton.....BILL KENWRIGHT
Holt................ROGER FERRY
Green..............EDWIN BROWN
Miss Nichols.....BRENDA COWLING
Alan............PAUL THOMPSON
Mrs Milton........BETTY ENGLAND

Series created by TED WILLIS
Design by DAPHNE SHORTMAN
Programme co-ordinator JOE WATERS
Produced by PHILIP BARKER †
(Peter Byrne is in 'There's a Girl in my Soup' at the Comedy Theatre)

7.30 *Colour*
The Harry Secombe Show
Appearing with Harry are
Lulu, Arthur Askey
Julian Orchard, Jonathan James
Written by JIMMY GRAFTON and STAN MARS
Orchestra directed by MALCOLM LOCKYER
Sound ALAN EDMONDS
Lighting RICHARD HIGHAM
Design by CHRIS THOMPSON
Produced by TERRY HUGHES
('Six-note falsetto giggle': page 22)

Radio Times
The Sixties 1969

RADIO TIMES 18/25 DECEMBER 1969

PAGE 104

polyfoto

Proof Sheet

Negative No AB 624

THE SIXTIES +++ HAIR DOWN, SKIRTS UP

Every time John Lennon appeared on television with his hair just that bit longer a million youngsters saw it, liked it, and copied it. Every time the pop-show cameras played lovingly on the thighs of Lulu or Sandie Shaw a million young girls reached for the scissors. Television was not in itself responsible for long hair and miniskirts, but it made sure everybody knew they had arrived.

Remember fashion in the early sixties? Men wore short back and sides and broad suits with jackets that barely covered their bottoms. Jean Shrimpton was wowing them in *Vogue* by courtesy of Bailey's photographs. All change was gradual, and if you took two steps in a particular direction instead of one at a time you were considered an exhibitionist. Then suddenly it all seemed to happen at once.

The origins of long hair and miniskirts are debatable. The Beatles used to say that their hair was combed forward because they tried it once for fun and it looked good: the logical development was then to let it grow into a fringe. The Rolling Stones took it from there, and took it to some considerable length.

Then the rest of us got in on the rebelling act and even the most conservative stockbroker is now allowed to have a few curls around the collar to go with his greying of the temples. And we all know about Hippies and *Hair*.

The first miniskirts to be shown in *haute couture* startled the world in 1964 when Courreges showed us his space-age collection. But it wasn't until the warm summer days of the following year that hems rocketed up, and then it happened not in Paris but in London.

Molly Parkin, fashion editor of *Nova* in those great days, thinks there was more to it than a simple shift of interest from bosoms. Democracy, she insists, had at last hit fashion. Up until then it was only starlets who had courage. But working girls were able to exploit short skirts for themselves. In 1965 alone the average rise in London was from just above the knee to four inches above the knee. And they continued to go up. This year the calculation of the really brave girls is done the other way round – from the bottom down.

There was more to it than democracy, of course. Any psychiatrist will talk about the miniskirt's associations with aggression, both social and sexual, and narcissism. But the real story of the miniskirt at the end of 1969 must be its obituary. When the sun comes out next spring it will be shining back on the bosom. Words by BILL SMITHIES

LET IT BE

As the 1960s drew to a close, the Beatles were on the brink of breaking up – and *Radio Times* looked back over a decade of changing fashions and John Lennon's hairstyles. *RT* correspondent Bill Smithies, at least, was braced for the 1970s...

The Planets
for kids

Texts
Cyril Blanchet

Illustrations
Cyril Blanchet & IA

Introduction

Welcome to the fascinating world of our solar system!

This book is an exciting journey through space. You'll learn about the unique characteristics of each planet, their position relative to the sun, and fun facts about them.

Through this book, you will discover the mysteries and wonders of the solar system in which we live.

Get ready to take off and explore space!

The 8 Planets

Mercury   **Venus**   **Earth**   **Mars**

Jupiter   **Saturn**   **Uranus**   **Neptune**

Interesting celestial objects

Sun   **Pluto**   **Moon**

Solar System

The solar system is a fascinating place in the universe. It is a place where everything revolves around the Sun. Celestial objects in the solar system include planets, stars, comets, and asteroids.

There are eight planets in our solar system, each with unique and interesting characteristics.

The solar system is very large and there is a lot to explore and discover.

Scientists are still studying a lot about our solar system, so there are always new discoveries to be made.

It is a fascinating place to explore!

Sun

The sun is an enormous ball of hot gas that sits in the center of our solar system. Without it, life on Earth would not be possible. It provides us with light and warmth, and all of the planets in our solar system orbit around it.

Fun fact

The sun is so massive that it makes up 99.8% of the entire mass of our solar system!!

Mercury

Mercury is the closest planet to the sun and it is the first planet in our solar system. It's small and rocky and its surface is covered in craters. It's not a good place to live because it's too hot during the day and too cold at night.

Fun fact

A day on Mercury (the time it takes for the planet to rotate once on its axis) is only about 58 Earth days long!

Venus

Venus is the second planet from the sun and it's the hottest planet in the solar system. It has thick clouds that trap heat and make the surface hot enough to melt lead. Venus also has volcanoes that can shoot lava high into the sky.

Fun fact

Venus is the brightest object in the night sky after the Moon!

Earth

Earth is the third planet from the sun and it's the only planet we know that can support life. It has oceans, mountains, deserts, and forests. People, animals, and plants live on Earth.

Fun fact
The Earth is not quite round like a perfect snowball, it has a slightly flattened top and bottom shape, like a deflated balloon! This is because of the force of the Earth's rotation causing it to stretch a little.

Mars

Mars is the fourth planet from the sun. It's often called the "Red Planet" because of its reddish appearance. It has mountains, valleys, and a huge canyon. There is also evidence that there might be water on Mars, and it might have been suitable for life long time ago.

Fun fact

There are signs that Mars might have had a warmer and wetter climate in the past, which could have supported life!

Jupiter

Jupiter is the fifth planet from the sun and it's the biggest planet in the solar system. It's mostly made of gas and has a big red spot on it that is a giant storm. Jupiter has 79 moons, the most of any planet in the solar system.

Fun fact

Jupiter's "Great Red Spot" is a giant storm that's been raging for at least 350 years!

Saturn

Saturn is the sixth planet from the sun. It's famous for its rings that are made of ice and rocks. It has at least 53 moons, the second most of any planet in the solar system.

Fun fact

Saturn's rings are made of ice and rocks and some of them are as big as mountains!

Uranus

Uranus is the seventh planet from the sun and it's also known as the "Ice Giant" because it's mostly made of gas and ice. It has 27 known moons and has unique feature because it's tilted on its side.

Fun fact
Uranus has the coldest atmosphere of any of the planets, with temperatures reaching as low as -371 degrees Fahrenheit!

Neptune

Neptune is the eighth planet from the sun and it's similar to Uranus but it's a deeper blue color. It has 13 known moons.

Fun fact

In 1989, a spacecraft called Voyager 2 flew by Neptune and took the first-ever close-up images of the planet!

Pluto

Pluto is no longer considered a planet but it's still interesting. It's a small, icy object that orbits the sun at the edge of our solar system. It has 5 known moons

Fun fact

Pluto was considered a planet for 76 years, but in 2006, it was reclassified as a "dwarf planet"!

Moon

The Moon is a big, gray rock that goes around Earth. We can see the moon in the night sky and it changes its shape over time. We call it new moon when its not visible from earth, crescent when its partially visible and full moon when we can see the whole moon. Moon does not give light itself, it reflects sunlight and that's how we see it in the night sky.

Fun fact

The Moon is about one-quarter the size of Earth and is the fifth-largest natural satellite in the Solar System.

About the author

Cyril Blanchet is a children's book author and AI illustrator based in Canada. With a focus on creative and colorful illustrations, Cyril creates books that both entertain and educate young readers.

His books are filled with imagination and wonder.

Cyril has a passion for spreading the love of reading to children and seeks to inspire a love for literature in young minds.

This book is dedicated to my children

Jules et Louise

If you enjoyed your reading, please leave a review on amazon

Printed in Great Britain
by Amazon